WHAT PEOPLE ARE SAYING ABOUT OPERATION TERRA

While you can find many books today on world transformation, *Operation Terra* is in a class by itself. Here you'll find clear words, deep ideas, and an unusually broad view of human soul growth and the Earth's own path. Whether you are new to the field, or you have already read dozens of New Age books, I think you'll be impressed with this book. I strongly recommend it, and I know you'll be pleased it came your way.

—Scott Mandelker, Ph.D., author of
From Elsewhere: Being ET in America, and
Universal Vision: Soul Evolution and the Cosmic Plan

A profound and extraordinary view of Terra, a new world on a new level of existence, written by a remarkable and gifted woman who has both seen it and heard it.

—Jeannie Seeley-Smith, Executive Director, Perspectives, Inc.
and author of *No One's in the Kitchen with Dinah:
How Working Couples Can Make It Work*

I have read widely in the fields of the Bible, near-death experience, the spiritual realms, spirituality, Marian Apparitions, ancient prophecy, and UFOs. Something is going on out there. The material shared by Lyara is an excellent synthesis of all that I have read. I am impressed that what I learned over many years from dozens of books is being offered by one source. Now is the time to pay attention.

—Rev. Richard A. Dinges

I love the message TERRA conveys. Thank you for making this book full of hope, strength and resourcefulness, as well as holding a promise to be fulfilled. It is written in a way that is real, understandable, and helpful to reconnect to the Source. The words "Let go—let God" have a particular alignment to this truthful gift of TERRA and redirects one's priorities to what is really important.

—Christa Dowling, Former Editor-in-Chief, VOGUE/Germany

The *Open Line* newspaper has used articles from this author because of the integrity of the information.

—LuAnn Stallcop, Editor & Publisher
Conley Enterprises, Spokane, Washington, USA

Operation Terra is a fantastic exploration into the new energies coming into our planetary sphere right now. The Messages contained in the *Operation Terra* material speak to the heart and soul of those seeking to advance their spiritual growth and join with others in loving and compassionate i███████████████████ highly recommended reading!

—████████ amics:
 olution

I don't know if events will transpire exactly the way the material says it will. All I know is that when I read it, it brought me to tears and touched my heart. I've been around long enough to know that when that happens, there has to be truth in it. I've also come to realize that ascension, for this planet and for myself, is the reason that I was born.

—Joseph Fazio, bus mechanic, USA

Operation Terra is a profound, loving gift to the reader, giving us insightful glimpses into our origins and our transition to living in perfect peace and harmony on Terra. I highly recommend this book to all who are on a spiritual path.

—K. J. Sluga, Environmental Services Director (retired), Wisconsin, USA

Every time I return to the *Operation Terra* Messages, I am struck afresh by their elevating profundity. Lyara is definitely tuned in to a high, clear frequency of loving, cosmic inspiration, and her painstaking presentation of the Messages she receives reflects her reverence for them, and for all who are attracted to them. I recommend them without hesitation to any who quest for a vision of Higher Love and Higher Wisdom. The Messages improve with repeated reading.

—J. Harmon Grahn, author and publisher, *The New Paradigm*;
co-originator, *Free Digital Library*

Having been involved with layman studies of general science, religion, and philosophy for many years including physics, metaphysics, and cosmology, I was quick to recognize the clarion ring of truth resonating forth from *Operation Terra*. This is truly an amazing and timely revelation at this Omega Point cosmic cycle of completion. It is one minute to midnight; the Creation is about to be entirely re-created, hence our spiritual practice must be our highest priority, as shown in *Operation Terra*.

—Werner Sohn, retired engineer, Massachusetts, USA

This work is essential reading and application for all who care about the destiny of Mother Earth. There is a lot of false and misleading material being channeled today, and *Operation Terra* resonates wholeheartedly with Truth, Wisdom, Light and Unconditional Love. Lyara presents *Operation Terra* without ego, which is a rare quality in spiritual authors of our time.

—Daniel Butt, England

The messages in *Operation Terra* will speak to your soul. This will be the experience you have been searching for your whole life, and by the end of this book you will be forever changed. Welcome to the Family... See you on Terra!

—Sherry Tapke, owner, Action Agency, Cincinnati, Ohio, USA

I have been a loyal visitor of the *Operation Terra* site since I returned from living in London, where I awakened to "what is going on" on this planet. It has been one of the few sites in which the material is always clear and incredibly relevant upon each step of the Earth's ascension and my own. The information holds energies resonant of a very high level of consciousness, which strikes a chord within my heart. I would like to thank Lyara for her wonderful work, which has given so many [people] clear guidance, insight, and a profound sense of security about what lies ahead."

—Ailie Freeland, Sydney, Australia

When I found this information, it brought me a lot of peace of mind and heart, and I also knew it was the right complement that my soul needed to complete my earthly preparation to achieve the fulfillment of the Divine Promise, that hope which my fathers died with.

—Agustin García Muñiz, Accountant
Guaymas, Sonora, México

Simply put, I was told of the *Operation Terra* site by a friend upon re-discovering my interest in ascension. Being moved by the sincerity of your work and words, she felt I would resonate with your message and its beauty. She was correct. It allowed me to journey with you from the beginning of the story to the present with a clear understanding of the message. I appreciate your clarity and personal response to my questions. You told me you had to be willing to be a "single point amongst the many points." That has certainly been true, and I understand that now more than ever. Thank you for your efforts to help us in our evolution and ascension of this physical experience into the next!

—Christina Clark, entrepreneur, USA

"Outstanding" and "beautiful" come to mind as I read OT! The angels who bring these Messages are very skilled at making the higher realms understandable to the 3D human mind. I greatly appreciate the timing of these Messages, as they prepare us for Terra's transition in a common-sense and loving manner. God is giving us ample information as to what is coming...are you listening?

—Tom Hernandez, USA

We have both been touched and uplifted by the purity, beauty, and harmony of the *Operation Terra* Messages. Our inner awareness confirms much of what has been expressed. We know there are many others who will also be inspired and reassured on hearing of such a magnificent vision of our future reality.

—Nick & Peggy, USA

Operation Terra touched my heart with its depth of love and understanding of the human condition. It opened that "all knowing" part of me I hadn't realised was there all the time.

—Annie Lee Best, poet, Cornwall, England

Beloved Lyara, in sharing her gifts as a celestial communicator, is making available timely and unprecedented information to assist all seeking ones in making the most vital choices ever open to human ones at any time in the history of the race. I am extremely grateful, and the way is opening up!

L. Dean Patterson, Ret. Navy officer (WWI);
owner/broker, New Horizons Real Estate, Oakhurst, California, USA

Everybody can see it: we live in a time in which everything is changing, and so we are changing, too. The Hosts of Heaven describe the way and the process through which Earth is changing from the material world of today into a much more spiritual world tomorrow—Terra—in a very detailed manner and what it means to us as the future inhabitants of Terra. I believe and trust in these wonderful Messages, and even more—I feel that they are true!

—Uli Flender, Germany

Operation Terra is channelings from the spiritual realm which describe in highest clarity the situation of our time and the developments towards a new Earth and her citizens. Those who experience these channelings as true within their hearts and resonate with them, are the targets. They learn about their destiny on the new Earth, "Terra." Other Earth-citizens will not be so happy with the Messages. They belong to other groups with other destinies. However all will recognize that these Messages fit seamlessly together with others, which speaks for their authenticity and their independence.

—Dr. Edgar Schättle, Frankfurt am Main, Germany

Operation Terra has provided insightful keys to many pieces of the greater puzzle, which activate the cellular levels in bringing forth their remembrance of origin, as the Atoms to the Adams for the Bio-genesis of the Greater Light. This is a "must read" message, delivered through its scribe, from the Universal Consciousness.

—Lee Guilmette Chin, Seattle, Washington, USA

I consider the *Operation Terra* website one of the most important on the Internet. The [Messages] all resonate well with me, and I have sent most of them to my mailing list. I will continue to look forward to future [Messages] from Lyara.

—Sue Potter, USA

Operation Terra has provided me with a view of a world that is our destiny. The words used have rung "True," deep in my soul. This is divinely inspiring material.

—Doug Crandall, The Barefoot Poet, USA

From the heart... This presentation of the Eternal Verities is the clearest and most concise I have ever read. Terra is my unfulfilled dream, which I recognize is mine to live at last.

—Josette de Pendragon, USA

OPERATION TERRA

MESSAGES FROM THE HOSTS OF HEAVEN

*A new revelation on Earth changes, ETs, the end times,
and the journey to the New Earth, Terra*

VOLUME ONE

SARA LYARA ESTES

CELESTIAL COOPERATIVES
Oroville, WA 98844
USA

OPERATION TERRA
MESSAGES FROM THE HOSTS OF HEAVEN
*A new revelation on Earth changes, ETs, the end times,
and the journey to the New Earth, Terra*

COVER ART, TYPOGRAPHY AND DESIGN BY SARA LYARA ESTES

ISBN 0-9711297-0-3

Library of Congress Control Number: 2001117583

CELESTIAL COOPERATIVES
PO Box 2231
Oroville, WA 98844-2231

Printed in the USA
on acid-free paper

Dedicated to
the Hosts of Heaven
and the Operation Terra family

ABOUT VOLUME TWO

As this book goes to press, Volume Two of the material is in the process of being received. Whereas Volume One lays the foundation, it is already apparent that Volume Two is going deeper and higher than Volume One—another turn on the spiral leading to Terra. If you would like to be notified when Volume Two is available in print, use a copy of the form on page 143 and the addresses shown on page 142 to request update information. If you change location, keep us apprised of your move(s) so we can reach you at the appropriate time.

You can also keep up with the changing Operation Terra scene by checking the Web site (www.operationterra.com) periodically and/or asking to be on the mailing list (send an e-mail to maillist@operationterra.com). Good journey!

ACKNOWLEDGMENTS

In truth, everything that has appeared in my life has brought me to where I am and to the writing of this book, so I thank ALL of my "teachers," whether you gave me a positive example or the other kind, because you all gave me the opportunity to see my Self in you. That being said, there are some individuals that I wish to acknowledge as special "teachers" for me of the positive kind:

My cousin Lois, who was the first to tell me that I was "counter-culture" (I didn't know what that meant except that nobody I ever voted for got elected!), and who showed me that material wealth could be handled responsibly and with sensitivity and generosity. Without her help, this book would not have been printed;

Lois's husband Manny, who was the first person I met who embodied heart-centered wisdom, and thanks go to both of them for their generosity, hospitality, and warm acceptance of me in my exploration of life;

My beloved partner Michael, who has been the most difficult teacher of all, but who has also supported me, nourished me, and gifted me in so many ways that they are beyond counting;

My friend Jon, who was a fellow traveler on the path during the time when I was most alone. He was unrelenting in his ferocious-ness for the truth and at all times held me accountable for the highest I was capable of;

Jan, who shared so many of the days of my awakening and reminded me to "lighten up" when I got too serious;

My father, who taught me that "doing the right thing" was more important than expediency, and gave me a solid sense of ethics on which to base my life;

My mother, who taught me a lot about what I did NOT want to be like, but who modeled a deep loyalty to her family and was also "there" for me in the ways I most needed her during the hard times;

Dr. Jacqueline Krohn, M.D. for guiding me back to functionality when I was disabled, for her courage, and for her willingness to tell me the truth about my situation so that I could come to terms with it and move on;

Rabbi Eric Greenbaum, my 8th grade Sunday school teacher, who was the first person I met that had transcended his religion, who told me that God was in all things, and who showed me that there are "saints" everywhere;

Charles P. Overton, Jr., my elementary school science teacher, who was the only teacher that encouraged me to make use of my intellectual abilities, and for showing me the magazine article about the metamorphosis of butterflies when I was 10 years old;

and to Meusch, Gretchen, Mom Cat, Speckles, Geronimo and Amador, who have taught me about life, birth, death, and love, as only animals can.

CONTENTS

FOREWORD. xv

INTRODUCTION xvii

THE MESSAGES FROM THE HOSTS OF HEAVEN

1: OPERATION TERRA. 21
☆ the elohim ☆ the interlopers ☆ the plan for Earth ☆ the New
Earth ☆ a unique definition of love ☆

2: ON BECOMING A "HUMAN" BEING. 25
☆ the Adamic race ☆ the life force vs. entropy ☆ the true
human ☆ using Love, Light, and sound for purification and
restoration ☆ symptoms of cleansing ☆ surrender and
acceptance ☆ you have so much help ☆

3: ON ROOTING OUT FEAR 33
☆ Earth changes ☆ tuning in to Source for your support
☆ fear vs. love ☆ the "Second Coming" ☆ the Big Lie ☆

4: SUPPORTING YOUR TRANSITION 37
☆ different exit paths and timelines ☆ differentiation and
resonance ☆ free will and soul choice ☆ the transformational
process ☆ things you can do to assist your transition ☆ setting
your priorities ☆ disconnect from the drama ☆

5: A GUIDED TOUR OF TERRA 43
☆ a visit to Terra ☆ seedpoints and fractals ☆ the evolutionary
spiral ☆

6: MERGING OF REALITIES 49
☆ decision points and logic branches ☆ Universal Laws ☆
parallel realities ☆ holograms ☆ the Alpha, the Omega, and
the Null Point ☆ you are the "seed" for a new "set" of
potentials ☆ the other "you"s are merging into your soul ☆

7: THE HARVESTING OF SOULS 57

☆ the Oversoul ☆ the silver cord ☆ simultaneous "lives"
☆ time defines location ☆ the experience of reality is totally
subjective ☆ Source is going to "blink" ☆ the harvesting of
souls ☆

8: ON PROBABILITIES 65

☆ the Creator likes surprises ☆ no one can know the future
with any degree of certainty ☆ the "gears" are lining up ☆ a
window of opportunity for an entirely new Creation ☆ Earth
changes are necessary ☆ 3 groups will be taken off the planet ☆

9: CHANGING INTO "GODS" 71

☆ holograms ☆ the Light Body ☆ you will have total Mastery ☆
you will change physically ☆ Let go and let God ☆ letting go
is the way through ☆

10: ON EXTRATERRESTRIALS AND THE HARVEST 75

☆ definition of "extraterrestrial" ☆ there are many ET races
interacting with Earth ☆ ETs come in two "flavors": STS and
STO ☆ the Creator just IS ☆ Harvest ☆ trust your feelings ☆

11: SUMMING UP 83

☆ Earth changes serve several purposes ☆ Archangel Michael
and the Hosts of Heaven ☆ in STO cultures, everything is
sovereign ☆ your first task is your own transformation ☆ you
are surrounded by angels ☆

12: SIGNS ALONG THE WAY 89

☆ darkness and light ☆ signs of the times ☆ honor and respect
your body ☆ supporting your process ☆ your true family ☆

13: IT'S ALL GOD 95

☆ nothing is outside of God ☆ Earth changes are necessary ☆
the new "plagues" ☆ the homecoming ☆ the new dawn ☆

14: THE CROSSING-POINT 101
     ☆ the expansion into a new reality ☆ merging with the
     Godhead ☆ absorbing more Light ☆ receive your birthright
     ☆ all souls are equal ☆

15: THE COMING STORM 105
     ☆ darkness is a lack of understanding ☆ making choices
     ☆ technology and economics are vulnerable
     ☆ the Earth and sun are players, too ☆ parallel futures ☆

16: ALLOW ALL THINGS 111
     ☆ intensification of the polarities ☆ allowing vs. fighting ☆
     definition of Mastery ☆ "resist not" ☆ on Terra, all will be
     sovereign ☆

17: THE NEW MILLENNIUM 115
     ☆ floating into the new reality ☆ trust the process ☆

18: THE SPLITTING OF THE WORLDS 119
     ☆ the intensification of essence ☆ the winds of change
     ☆ disengaging from what is not "yours" ☆ you are pioneers
     ☆ walking into the dream ☆

19: THE BOTTOM LINE 125
     ☆ recap of earlier Messages ☆ the present Earth will "pass
     away" ☆ only love, peace and joy will exist on Terra
     ☆ what to do in the meantime ☆ erasing cellular memory ☆

ANSWERS TO FREQUENTLY ASKED QUESTIONS. 131
     ☆ how will we know... ? ☆ frequency bands ☆ density and
     dimension ☆ coming back ☆ not like Heaven's Gate ☆

SUGGESTED READING 139
ABOUT THE AUTHOR 141
ABOUT THE PUBLISHER / CONTACT INFORMATION. 142
ORDER FORM, REQUEST FOR UPDATES 143

And it shall come to pass afterward, that I will pour out my spirit upon ali flesh; and your sons and your daughters shall prophesy, your old men shall dream dreams, your young men shall see visions;

And also upon the servants and upon the handmaids in those days will I pour out my spirit.

Joel 2:28-29

FOREWORD

Back in 1952, a time when trusting spiritual guidance from the other side of the veil was rare and risky, my wise unseen teacher said that within 30 years the word "channeling" would be commonplace, if not entirely accepted. And, he cautioned, be very careful in discerning what was being said before accepting it at face value.

Well, nearly 50 years have passed. The prediction has come true, and the prudent counsel for maintaining personal discernment remains valid.

A parallel to the early days of radio is appropriate here. Once there were only a handful of broadcasting stations—and a handful of listeners. Today there are thousands of stations. Which do you listen to? Which ones carry the information, music, and news that are useful? As we have learned, simply being able to broadcast is no assurance of worthiness of our attention.

How can an individual discern integrity and draw value from the babble of present day channeling? A fair question.

As you read any spiritual materials, go within. Listen not only with your mind—which is clogged with worldly manipulation and programming dating from earliest childhood. Listen with your heart. Yes, this advice runs contrary to our conditioning, but it works! Ours is a society that values mental abilities far above an open and loving heart.

Read these Messages using not only your intellect but your intuition, or as some like to call it, your Inner Knower. Free of judging phrases, free from religious-command overtones, the Messages come across as a dialog with a wise older friend, or an astute author (albeit not incarnate) of a self-help book who has a loving intent to educate.

Lyara's source is literate, thoughtful and provocative. The communications focus on content, on ideas that expand the vision and the heart. There is no request to persuade to a personal viewpoint.

Here are four useful questions to test the integrity in a piece of "channeled" information: Is the channeled source asking you to just accept as fact what is being said? Is your attention being focused on a non-physical personality that claims to be wiser, grander or better than you? Is there a request for worship of the speaker or the speaker's philosophy? And of course, check out whether the message contains the ever-popular doom-and-gloom viewpoint, or does it uplift and inspire you?

The name "Operation Terra" has military overtones—and perhaps in some ways the image is apt. To organize and inspire the evolution of a planet with six billion souls on it requires a level of order and staffing one might find in a well-run military campaign. Pragmatically, the real questions at the end of the day are: Do you intuitively feel the rightness of the information? Is your awareness of the larger life beyond 3D Earth now more comfortable for you?

If any idea does not quite feel right, instead of tossing it aside, place it into the basket of something to look into another time and let it go. It's been my experience that Creator will find a fresh way to present a truth again to you in a more palatable form. Nothing will have been lost by the delay.

So I suggest you read Lyara's transmissions and make up your own mind and heart whether this data is worthy of your attention and your belief. You are the only fit judge for this decision.

Ronald S. Ross
former publisher, The New Age Press

Ronald S. Ross has served as Managing Director and Principal for two national consulting firms and Chief Executive Officer of a public company. A frequent speaker at national and regional conferences on the transforming role of the individual in our consolidating world economy. Ronald is proudest of his quiet 40 year career as an educator, lecturer and author on matters spiritual and metaphysical.

INTRODUCTION

The journey that led up to the publishing of this book was a long and difficult one. Like the Messages themselves, each step in that journey built upon the ones that had gone before and at the same time laid a foundation for future steps. If you want to get the most benefit from the material in this book, begin at the beginning and read the Messages in order, just as they were received.

These Messages were first offered to the world through the medium of the Internet, beginning on June 30, 1999. My original impulse had been to create a Web site through which I could share my personal views about what I saw was "wrong" with the world around me. However, at the moment my fingers were poised over the keyboard to begin, my "upstairs team" sounded a tone in my right ear—their signal to me to "pick up my inner telephone" and to hear what they had to say.

I always cringe a little when this happens, as I do not enjoy receiving criticism, and they usually offer me more of that (in an indirect way) than praise. I refer to these loving admonishments as "course corrections," which I am not entirely thrilled to receive, but for which I am ultimately very grateful, for they do keep me "on track" and appropriately humbled in my seeking. When a former acquaintance remarked with some envy that I seemed to receive constant guidance, whereas she (who asked often) got so little, my truthful reply to her was, "It keeps me from walking into walls."

I mention this because it is easy for people to read these Messages and then expect me to answer for them, as if I were some expert on the bigger picture behind them. I have been "in training" for more than 20 years now, ever since Christ called me to this solitary path. I do have some skill as a conduit for these Messages, and can reply intelligently and in depth as to the content of the transmissions that I receive, but I am walking the same walk of faith and trust that everyone else is. I never know when the next Message will come or even if there will be another one at all.

On June 28, 1999, the guidance I received was as follows: "We suggest that, instead of focusing on the world that is dying, you offer a vision of hope that people can carry with them to sustain them in the days ahead." From the vision I had received in 1982, I knew exactly what was meant by "the days ahead," and I resonated with that intent immediately. In that moment, the vision of *Operation Terra* was born, although I still did not know exactly how I would proceed with it. Two days later, they "rang my ear" again, and this time they made a specific request: "Would you be willing to deliver a series of Messages for us and to share them with others?" In all of my years of training, I had never been asked to share any of the material with anyone else. This would be another step out on the limb for me, another step of deeper faith in the unseen and the continued willingness to "put my neck up to the knife" in the service to which I am called.

For those who have never "channeled," a little explanation might be helpful here. I am at heart a recluse. I am much more comfortable "hiding" than being on the stage, although I do confess that the few times I have been on the stage I have largely enjoyed it (childhood piano recitals being the exception!). To be a good channel, one must open oneself up in a way that does not allow one to "preview" or "edit" what comes through. One must train one's ego to step aside and be willing to say whatever is presented, even if it might be "wrong" or "crazy," or any number of other fear-based labels about how it will be perceived/received by others.

In "conscious channeling," one's personality is still present, and it is very easy to succumb to the temptation to alter the words to fit one's own personal perspective. There is no way to separate the source of the material from the personality of the channel. There is no such thing as a "100% pure" channel, and so those of us who do this work have to take certain risks in being willing to bring through information from sources that are invisible to us and to hope that what we bring through is of high quality and serves a positive purpose.

This is further complicated by the fact that there are entities on other planes, and even "psi-ops" by other humans who are being used as tactical weapons behind the scenes, that seek to infiltrate a channel and to feed through disinformation, with the aim of discrediting the channel and sowing confusion in the listener, so that the result is skewed to their particular agenda. It takes constant "testing" and discernment to discriminate as to when something feels "off," and it is a very tricky business indeed to attempt to do this with any degree of purity. In the end, one has to surrender up ALL attachments, even to being "right" or "good." As one's skills mature and one's spiritual opening progresses, the material deepens accordingly, and I can see that in my own work, as well. That is how evolution proceeds.

I am often asked about how I receive this information. I am fully conscious and fully present, although in a deeply altered state, which I have trained myself to enter at will. The transmission comes in as a stream of impressions, which I perceive with all of my subtle senses. They are "felt" and experienced, rather than heard as "words in my head," but I can tell what is meant; if I'm not sure, I may try a different word to convey the meaning, and can then tell which one is the right one (usually the first one I got). The written words are carrier waves for the Light codes that accompany them. When you read the words (and if you are open to receive them), the Light codes stream into you and activate your cellular codes and the remembrance of the information they contain.

The Messages presented here are exactly what came through, to the best of my ability to translate the telepathic impress. I offer them with an open hand and an open heart. If they speak to you, you will know it in *your* heart, even if your mind has many questions. If they seem like just so many words on a page to you, or you can't tell the qualitative difference between this material and so much else that is out there, then perhaps this isn't "yours," and your path is somewhere else. No blame—either for you or for me.

There is a great sorting out taking place, and these Messages are intended for those whose souls have chosen the journey to Terra as their next step on the path back to Source. If these words speak to *your* heart, then welcome to the family! We are gathering and we will share in this future of Terra together. If not, then God wants something else for your life, and I bless you and your path in getting there. We are all Love-in-action and God-in-expression, so no path is better than any other path. They are just presenting different scenes along the way.

"...the harvest is the end of the world;
and the reapers are the angels."
Matthew 13:39

1

OPERATION TERRA
June 30, 1999

IN THE BEGINNING, this planet was created with a certain destiny path in mind. Its creators (the "elohim," a group of vast, intelligent beings who combined forces to create this sector of reality) envisioned a rich environment where the planet's theme of "seeking harmony in diversity" could play out. However, there were other beings that saw an opportunity to insert themselves into the paradigm and eventually did so, so successfully that the original blueprint for the planet was essentially abrogated and converted to another agenda entirely.

Every time the elohim would project expressions of themselves into the physical plane and try to restore the original plan and agenda, the interlopers would eventually undermine their efforts and redirect the planet toward their own aims and ambitions. The world you see around you is the result of this interaction. A relatively few individuals adhere to the original standards, based on love for and responsibility toward the entire planet and its occupants, but many more individuals put their own interests above those of the whole and engage in destructively competitive behaviors that eventually harm everyone and everything.

Now, however, it is time to restore the planet to her original destiny path. The behaviors that have destroyed so much of her diversity and beauty will be put to an end. Those who can "hear" these words will save much more than themselves. They will be candidates for the opportunity to inhabit the Earth after she has risen to her glorified state, the "New Earth," Terra, and they will be active participants WITH THE PLANET in creating a "heaven" on Earth.

In a relatively short time from now, many things will begin playing out that were prophesied to occur sooner, but had been delayed so that the message for change could reach the greatest number of potential "recruits." Now, however, all must go forward in order for the planet to meet her appointment with her own destiny.

All things have a proper time. "To every thing, there is a season" is a good way to put it, and right now it is almost autumn, the time to harvest what has been sown. Each lifeform has had many thousands of years to perfect itself and to evolve to its present state. Many species are simply leaving because there is no longer support for them to remain here. Drastic action is needed now, if anything is to be preserved.

The planet does not need its lifeforms. There are many planets without anything above the mineral kingdom. It is total arrogance on the part of even the best-intentioned humans to speak of "saving the planet." The planet can get along just fine on her own. But the planet is a conscious being, and the soul of the planet made an agreement as part of its incarnation as a physical reality. It agreed to host a diversity of lifeforms, and to interact with and sustain those lifeforms, in keeping with the planet's own destiny path. To this end, she has allowed much abuse of her body while patiently waiting for humans to "get" the message of what they were doing to that which sustains them.

Without Earth's water, air, and soil, there would not be any life at all. Even viruses and bacteria need water. Everything needs physical nurturance until it is able to manifest its needs directly from the underlying matrix of consciousness that supports and informs physical reality. But humans, in their blind pursuit of their own survival regardless of the cost, have inadvertently been destroying the very matrix that gives them life and sustains them. The human species has placed itself in competition with everything else on the planet—animals, plants, trees, birds, fish, and other humans—and has robbed, raped, and pillaged the very planet upon which they depend for everything.

Everything humans consume or use comes from the planet, be it food, clothing, oxygen, shelter, automobiles, or computers. All of the materials that are used to manufacture all of the goods that people use come from the planet. And yet the slaughter goes on, as the oceans are poisoned, the forests are felled, and the water is pumped out of the ground when local rainfall is not sufficient to support people's needs. Unless this is stopped, there will be nothing left, and the people will suffer a terrible, slow decline, as they fight with one another over ever-dwindling resources. Too few care. The lawmakers serve their own agendas; there is simply not enough of a force for change to matter at this late date in the process.

So now, we give you this warning and we also give you a promise. For those of you who can "hear," know that the ticket is love in your heart. By love, we do not mean the mushy, romanticized stuff of your movies and novels. By love, we mean the absence of fear, trust in the Creator, and a willingness to put one's life on the line for the truth. In a very short time now, those traits are going to be the only ones that gets one the "ticket to ride." A great wave of change is building now that will soon sweep the petty affairs of humans away, a great wave of purification and the cleansing of everything that is not in alignment with the destiny of this planet.

The elohim are here. They have incarnated as ordinary humans in order to act as human lightning rods, to draw down and anchor the energy of change, and to assist in the birthing of the new age. It will be necessary to evacuate those who are destined to inhabit Terra, for the necessary cleansing will render the present body of Earth uninhabitable for a time. The evacuees will be taken in their physical bodies to another location, where they will prepare themselves for the colonization of Terra, the "New Earth." The remainder of this information will deal with the details of that process and paint a vision that those who can "hear" will be able to hold in their hearts and minds and that will help them to understand the necessity of the cleansing that is soon to take place.

Amen, Adonoy Sabayoth. We are the Hosts of Heaven.*

---

* **NOTE:** The phrase "Adonoy Sabayoth" is a shortened version of "Kadosh, kadosh, kadosh, Adonoy Sabayoth," which is Hebrew for "Holy, holy, holy (is the) Lord of Hosts." This particular spelling is a transliteration that reflects the Hebrew dialect and pronunciation I was raised with, and differs from the more widely accepted "Adonai Tsebayoth." This term is used throughout the Messages as a sort of "seal of authenticity" by my sources, to certify that what I have received is indeed from them.

Many people have asked me who the Hosts of Heaven are. They have variously referred to themselves as being "your brothers and sisters in the many mansion worlds of the One Infinite Creator," the "angelic hosts" and "Legions of [Archangel] Michael," and the Hosts referred to in the expression "Lord of Hosts." They reside in the frequency bands "... that contain those you would call Masters, angels, and archangels," and "work with the Office of the Christ." (That is not a particular person, but an office or position within the spiritual hierarchy.)

2

ON BECOMING A "HUMAN" BEING
July 1, 1999

What people have come to think of as a human being actually is a hybrid creature, born of the manipulations of the interlopers. In the beginning, the Adamic seed was created whole and fully formed. It was designed to act as a steward of whatever world it found itself upon. To this end, it had the power of reason and the power to love and care for things other than itself. It had a unique genetic pattern that also allowed it full access to the higher dimensions and the wisdom contained in the *Akasha*, or Hall of Records.

The interlopers were originally from this same seed but a perversion crept in. Somehow the ability to love and care for others became distorted and replaced by a sense of disconnection that resulted in fear. In this fearful state, everything and everyone became perceived as an enemy, someone or something that posed a threat and therefore had to be controlled or dominated.

From this original distortion of the design for the Adamic race, a dark spiral began to unfurl and to block and interfere with the Light from Source Creator. It began to spread itself through the many worlds of the Father, and wherever it went, this distortion created chaos.

The life force is principally an ordering force. It acts against the tendency toward entropy. In any system, if some energy is not sustaining the system, it will dissolve and return to a more elemental state. In all systems, there is an ordering force or there would not be form. The evolutionary imperative is toward more complexity, toward more complex systems. The force of entropy is counter-evolutionary. It moves away from complexity toward simpler forms. In this sense, one can see the ordering force and the force of entropy as tending to oppose and balance each other. Since we have dubbed the ordering force as a life force, we can think of the force of entropy as a "death force" or "death wish," as all is consciousness and thought creates.

If we now look at the actions of the interlopers, we can see that they oppose the life force. Their principal activity sows dissent, competition instead of cooperation, and generally leads to a breakdown of any system that they penetrate successfully. They perceive of "self above all" as their guiding tenet, whereas the Adamic seed was designed to place self WITHIN the context of "all."

The Creator designed the Creation to reflect the Creator. The Creator is the source of the life force, the ordering principle that operates on the matrix of Mind and gives it form. The interlopers have distorted the original design, and we have been given the task of restoring all things to their original Divine estate. In the case of Earth, at this point in time that means to restore both the planet and its lifeforms to their original destiny plan—to their original evolutionary path.

The true human is a special case in the Creation. It shares many aspects with the Creator. If the Earth is in keeping with her blueprint, she will soon manifest as "The Garden" of the galaxy. And the true humans will act as her "Gardeners," in keeping with their stewardship role. Since Operation Terra is intended to restore Earth to her true destiny path, it follows that the so-called human beings must also be restored to theirs—to become true humans.

What does this mean? To understand the answer to this, one must look at what has changed. The DNA, which carries the codes for the operation of all the bodily processes, must be restored and elevated back to its original frequency of Light. The "shadows" cast by the interlopers must be cleansed and purified out of the system, and all of the entropic thoughtforms of separation, disease, and dying must be cleansed from the cellular memory patterns, which are carried in the DNA. Those portions of the DNA that were rendered inactive will have to be restored to full functionality, which carries with it the gift of full consciousness. If one could see the Light Bodies of animate forms, one would also see a web of infinitely delicate Light fibers interconnecting all things, all the way back to the Source. These connections funnel in through the subtle energy channels of the body—the *meridians* of acupuncture and the *chakras* and *nadis* of the Sanskrit-based languages and cultures.

To restore these energy channels to full function requires a purification. The source of this is the application of certain frequencies of sound and Light to gradually repair the "dropped connections." While it is true that there are many healers using the technologies of sound and Light, the kind of "remedy" needed to restore all the lifeforms of Earth (including the human beings) is beyond the ability of even the most gifted healers. The scope of the "operation" is simply too large for any individual or organization to provide. There is a time coming when an even greater amount of Light and sound will be available than has been in the past. The effect of this will be to shake loose anything that is not resonant with the original blueprint for the planet and all the lifeforms upon her. You have perhaps become familiar with "ultrasonic cleaning." This is a good metaphor for the process.

In ultrasonic cleaning, a piece of dirty jewelry is placed in a bath of cleaning solution. High-frequency sound waves move through the solution, shaking the dirt loose but leaving the jewelry intact. It's a very precise and safe method, as it does not disturb anything but the dirt that is encrusted on the jewelry.

Every lifeform is a jewel in the crown of the Creator. An order has gone forth through the Creation that the original blueprint must be restored. Accordingly, every aspect of the Creation that is not in keeping with its original blueprint will be restored. In this case, the distortions are being "bathed" in Love and high-frequency sound is being used to shake loose all the accumulated "dirt" that is keeping the jewel from reflecting the Creator's Light.

The energy from Source is too powerful to be used directly. It must be "stepped down" through a series of "lenses" or "transformers," much as your household electric current is stepped down through a series of transformers to a level that can be used by your household appliances. So it is with this process. The energy is stepped down until it is at a level that can accomplish the desired result without destroying the target altogether.

We entitled this message, "On Becoming a 'Human' Being." We chose this title so that you, the reader, could understand what is happening to you. You and every lifeform on the planet have been receiving a "bath" of Love for many years now. It has gradually increased, in a geometric fashion, over a long period of time. If you are familiar with geometric curves, you will know that the effects are at first almost insignificant, but as the powers build upon one another, each step up the spiral becomes more and more pronounced. For example $2 \times 2 = 4$ and $2 \times 2 \times 2 = 8$, or twice the first step. From 4 to 8 is not a big change. But after only 8 steps, the total is 256, an increase of 128 times the original number. The next step is 512, then 1024, and so on. You can see that the changes at the beginning were relatively small, but then each successive step becomes more massive. If you were to plot this on a curve, at a certain critical point, the curve would go almost straight up, toward infinity.

This is where you are at the time of this Message. You are within the "critical zone" and the amount of energy streaming over you is increasing so rapidly that you can't help but notice the effects. If you watch your TV or read your newspapers and magazines, everything seems to be purring along, "business as usual." There are some "bumps in the road," such as school children taking up guns and killing other school children, peculiar weather patterns, droughts, wildfires, and intense storms. But what doesn't make the news are the subtle changes in the entire substrate. The reason the killings take place is that they are a SYMPTOM of what is really going on. Everything that is not in keeping with the original blueprint is being flushed out of the Earth system. These behaviors are SYMPTOMS of the underlying patterns of death and disease that have operated "under cover" for a very long time. This is coming to an end, but it will all surface as it leaves the system, just like one sees the pus coming out of an abscess when it finally opens up and heals itself from beneath the surface.

People have begun to notice that something strange is going on. Perhaps they are afraid to talk about it, or they busy themselves with activities that take their minds off of it. They distract themselves and worry about this or that, but the real worry is deep under the surface, gnawing at them. "What is going on?" they wonder, but they don't speak of this with others, so they don't know that others are experiencing the same thing. Your media looks for different ways to ENTERTAIN you. Remember the Romans? "Bread and circuses." That's how they kept the general populace from becoming restless. They were kept fed and entertained. But the Roman circuses were not the stuff of clowns and cotton candy. They pitted human against human, human against animal. It is not so different today.

But now that will not be sufficient. With the increase in Light and sound, things are going to get pretty intense—so intense that the entertainment will fade into the background as people struggle to cope with the enormous wave of change that is sweeping the planet. It shows up a little in the rate of change in your computer technology, but that is only a tiny glimpse of the degree of change that is now occurring. And as we said before, this is a geometric progression. It is a spiral that will take in more and more as it turns faster and faster.

Some will refuse to change. You have all known someone that would "rather fight than switch." They will resist change to such an extent that they would literally rather DIE than change. Many will make this choice. Know that when you see this happen, it isn't anyone's "fault." It was their plan all along. Their soul had made that decision before it came into their body. They are simply going to go out of this body and eventually take up another, so that they can continue with their "lessons." No big deal. You've all been doing that for a very long time, also.

Others have been embracing change for many years. They have learned the lesson of "surrender." Instead of "fighting," they have decided to ACCEPT the direction of their life and have decided to ACCEPT the consequences of that choice. No blame. You haven't seen them on TV. They aren't in *People* magazine. They are pretty invisible, but they are nearly ready to make their appearance on the world stage. They have been preparing for this for a long time, so they will be among the first to manifest the "true human" form. They will be helping others to ACCEPT the necessity of change and to make as grace-full (i.e. filled with Grace) a transition as possible.

The amount of Love that is available to you is staggering. There are so many beings on all levels of the Creator's kingdom that are massed to assist you in this transition. They are holding the portals open so that more and more Love is stepped down through their hearts to yours. If you could see them and know how many there are assisting you, you would be overcome with emotion at the idea that you were somehow worthy of such a gift. That is because of the shadows within you that have convinced you of your smallness, of your powerlessness. The interlopers made you that way so they could use you for their purposes.

But you are a true jewel in the crown of the Creation. We have come to provide the high-frequency sound to shake you loose of all that keeps you from shining forth and perfectly reflecting the Creator's Light. We are bathing you in a virtual ocean of Love. All you need to do is to SURRENDER and ACCEPT the gift. You will have to "die" to your idea of how small and powerless you are in order to become a "true human." You will have to ACCEPT the information that begins to flood into you as your Light filaments become reconnected to the Source. You will have to deal with your feelings when you discover how much of what you thought was important was part of the "Big Lie." But you have so much help. "Let go and let God" is a good phrase to express the degree of surrender that you must achieve.

We have defined love as the lack of fear, trust in the Creator, and the willingness to put your life on the line for the truth. We ask you now to move into your true estate, based on that definition of love, to allow yourselves to cast off your shame and guilt and receive the love that you are. We are here to help you.

Amen, Adonoy Sabayoth. We are the Hosts of Heaven.

If you bring forth what is within you, what you bring forth will save you. If you do not bring forth what is within you, what you do not bring forth will destroy you."

Gnostic Gospel of St. Thomas

3

ON ROOTING OUT FEAR
July 2, 1999

In this Message, we will attempt to paint a picture of what is currently playing out on Planet Earth. There is a mixture of energies, due to the workings of the interlopers. We have been assigned the task of separating them out from one another and making sure that each one gets to their proper "destination." If you see strange things happening—what you might call "miracles"—you will know that we are at work behind the scenes.

The weather patterns have already shifted dramatically, You can see this in the droughts, floods, hurricanes, and odd seasonal weather. However, that is nothing more than the planet's expression of ridding herself of all the negativity she has absorbed from the actions and thoughts of the humans who occupy her. She is merely "shaking herself loose" of the accumulated debris of human activity so that she can herself rise in frequency to meet her own appointment with destiny.

She will begin to "shake" in others ways, too. She is going to develop a "fever," with the aid of the sun, and that fever will do the same thing on the planetary surface as does a fever in a human being or an animal. The purpose of a fever is to burn off any foreign invaders (in the human/animal case, these would be the bacteria or viruses or foreign proteins of any kind) and to restore balance, or homeostasis. The weather patterns are the first symptoms of the Earth's disease process beginning to clear itself.

There will be other symptoms of this process, as well. There will be eruptions of the volcanic and geothermal type, just as boils appear on the surface of one's skin to eliminate toxins. There will be earthquakes as the Earth shudders herself free of the accumulated strains along the interfaces of her various parts. There will be massive bombardment of solar emanations, as well as the effects of a band of energy that your solar system has begun to transit. All of these things will be working together to provide the cleansing and purification that is needed, in order that the Earth may rise and achieve her station as Terra.

In these times, everything on the Earth will suffer the effects. There will not be any way to avoid it. Those who for now have artificial means of protecting themselves will soon see the loss of those means. Everything and everyone will be affected. However, there will be help for those who go within and find their security there. Inside of each of you, there is a center that allows you to connect with Source. It is more felt than seen, as it is invisible to the physical senses, but it is there. Those who meditate know what this feels like. It is not localized in any one part of the body. Rather, it is a feeling of expansion and comfort. If you do not meditate, now is a good time to start. Simply follow your breath as is goes in and out, and if your mind wanders, gently bring it back to the breath. You do not need any more technique than this. It helps if you meditate in the same place and at the same times every day, so it becomes a habit to go within. In this way, you will be able to not only receive the guidance or sense of what is yours to do, but you will also be positioning yourself to begin to receive the new information that will start to come in as your Light fibers are reconnected.

Remember, there is nothing you can do to prepare yourself for what is coming. If you think you are in charge, you will cut yourself off from the flow of information that comes from a higher source. Your own ego is programmed for the survival of your body. It is stimulated by fear. Your meditation practice is the place where you can find a "safe place" in which you need simply to listen. You cannot prepare for something that you don't know will come.

You don't know when or where or how you will need to cope with these coming Earth changes. If you are connected to Source, you will be led in what to do. If you are being run by your fear, you will make poor choices, and you will reap what you sow in that you will experience everything that you fear. You will draw it to yourselves through the principle of resonance.

So, then, have we frightened you? That is good. As soon as a fear rises to your consciousness, that is your opportunity to trace it back to its roots and "uproot" it. This is your part of the bargain, your part of the work. If you remember, we defined love as the absence of fear, trust in the Creator, and the willingness to lay down your life for the truth. All of these go hand in hand. You are either in fear or you are in love. You must make this choice over and over again, in each moment that presents. When a birth is taking place, the labor pains come closer and closer together as the moment of actual birth approaches. As we have said, you have now reached the critical point in which the rate of change will spiral upward exponentially. So remember to breathe. Give your meditation time or "quiet time" the highest priority, so that you can begin to eradicate those fears that you have left. Only those with love in their hearts—not fear—will be lifted. The vibration of fear will not be compatible with the new Earth, Terra. There will be no death, disease, or aging on Terra. All of those things are the result of unexpressed fear.

The ultimate fear is the fear of death. Despite the abundant testimony of those who have been "to death's door" and returned to tell about it, the fear of death underlies every other fear you have. Many subtle fears are tied to the idea of being socially unacceptable in one way or another. This subtly equates with ostracism, which in primitive cultures can lead to death from starvation or the lack of community support. This fear vanishes when you feel "connected" to Source. You carry within you the necessary comfort and faith, so that you are not swayed by outer appearances. Find others of like mind if you can, and perform group meditations on a regular basis. They will help you in strengthening the feeling of being part of a larger movement, a movement back to Source.

We have spoken of the interlopers and how they interfered

with the plan for this planet and everything upon her. These simple practices will remove you from the blind acceptance of the results of what they have done. It may not look or feel like you are doing much, but this is the ultimate rebellion. Those who are angrily demanding change from their government are placing their efforts in the wrong direction. You are perhaps familiar with the doctrine, "As above, so below." The second part of that is "As within, so without." If you want your world to be a safe place for you, you must first create your safety within yourself. Note that the change must occur "within" you before it is reflected "without" (outside of you).

You each have the potential to become warriors for the truth. The truth is that you do not need to die, that you CAN live a long and productive life that fulfills you in every way, and that you have never been and never will be separate from Source. The Christ has never left you, either, and so he cannot "return." This waiting for the "coming" that is present in all traditions throughout your world is really an expression of the sense of being cut off, of not being connected. The "coming" is about YOU, your coming back into the awareness of who you really are (an expression of the Creator) and coming back into your own true nature and estate. You are the "Second Coming," because you are destined to return or "come back" to what you were before. All the feelings that you must have a savior who is somehow out of reach is part of the Big Lie. There is only one Source. There is only ONE LIFE being lived, through each aspect of the Creation. You are both a part of and contain the whole of the Creator. The Creator can be accessed within yourself, and when you have achieved union with the Creator, you will know who you are.

We leave you now in peace and honor and blessing, and shall speak to you again.

Amen, Adonoy Sabayoth, We are the Hosts of Heaven.

4

SUPPORTING YOUR TRANSITION
July 3, 1999

Today's Message is about the different exit paths that will lead out of this one shared reality that you view as your home. It is true that you all see one picture now, but gradually this will change. It will not be noticeable at first, but it shall become increasingly amplified with the passage of time.

The greatest number of people will pass through the portal you call physical death. It is not true that they "die," but that is what it looks like to those who remain behind in the third dimension. They simply pass out of their bodies onto a different plane of reality that is normally invisible to those on "the other side" of the boundary between the planes.

For the rest, the experience will be somewhat different. A relatively small number will meet the criteria for moving on to Terra. Those are the ones that we will evacuate in their physical bodies. The others will think that they are still living on the same planet, but there will be a splitting off of realities, so that different timelines appear. To each person on a given timeline, it will seem as though a lot of people have simply disappeared. However, so much will be going on at the phenomenal level, that even this apparent disappearance will scarcely be noticed. They will be far too busy dealing with the challenges of moment-to-moment life. We are going to only speak of the experience for those who are destined for Terra. That is our concern in these Messages, although it is to be understood that the audience to whom we speak is very, very small.

A linkup is beginning to occur between those individuals who share a common destiny path. This is true for all of the different timelines. Through the principle of resonance, each "finds their own," so to speak. Each person will find that they are meeting total strangers with whom they instantly feel at home. With others, even ones who have been familiar in the past, it will be as if you are suddenly speaking different languages.

In fact, you are. Language is symbolic, and different cultures have different symbol systems. Each group will differentiate more and more from the others. It will be experienced as a "pull" or a "push." You will either feel attracted to certain individuals or you will feel a disconnect taking place with other individuals. You will either "like" them or you will feel anything ranging from mild disinterest to strong dislike. You will not be totally neutral toward anyone. Even though there is only ONE LIFE being lived, there is still the aspect of the uniqueness of each expression of that one life, and therefore there are certain tendencies to group in larger "families," rather than to identify with all people at the same time.

The people who are destined to go to Terra will resonate strongly with these Messages. Underneath the words, there is a strong vibratory signature that will trigger a response of "true" from within oneself, even if one does not totally comprehend all that is being said. You will either find yourself saying "Yes!!!!" or you will be repulsed. There is no in-between.

Those that are destined for Terra will be drawn to this material in three waves. The first of these is made up of the leadership, those who made a soul decision to be among the architects and builders of the new world. They are equipped by their souls for the task. *All of these decisions are made at the soul level*. We cannot stress that too strongly. One does not "earn" the right to go to Terra. One has chosen it as part of their soul's desired arena of expression and experience. True "free will" only exists at the soul level, where all is already known. To ask a blindfolded person to chart their course would be ridiculous, and everyone in a body who has not achieved a permanent state of Union with the Creator is essentially blindfolded. Only those who are fully awakened to and aligned with their soul can know the wisdom of the choices they make. You are not yet fully conscious, but you will be before this transition phase is complete.

To make the trip to Terra, all that is NOT of the proper vibratory level will be expelled from you. As you are raised in frequency, you will naturally be able to access more and more of the higher levels of existence. This will seem strange when it begins to happen, because the higher realities are not at all as "solid" as the one you are used to in your present form. They are a lot more "fluid," in that there are no solid boundaries. If you have ever read a good piece of stream-of-consciousness writing or had a lucid dream in which every conscious thought affected what you experienced as your environment, then you have some idea of what we are talking about.

So you will experience two separate and simultaneous processes—the expulsion of all that is NOT compatible with Terra and the unfoldment of the sorts of experiences that make up the moment-to-moment way of doing things at the next level of reality. They will seem rather strange to you at first, but if you can remember to breathe (and keep breathing) and to keep letting go of all your ideas about reality, you will have an easier time of it.

On Terra, you will operate with "beginner's mind." You will create in an "as-you-go" manner, with no real reference to what has gone before and no real plan of where you intend to go. Each action is both a result of the one just before it and the seed of the one that will follow. Each moment contains within it everything needed for its completion, but it is an experience of constant movement without any external referent to tell you which way you are going. Your entire process will be one of creating your reality without anything but curiosity to lead you. It will be as if there is an invisible finger always beckoning to you, "this way, this way." And you will go that way without hesitation, because you will have a perfect internal sense of it feeling "right" to do so. You will not question where it leads or what the consequences will be. You will be a fully-conscious, fully-trusting point of awareness that is always discovering itself in the moment, with no fixed idea of who it is or what it is supposed to be doing.

In some ways that is not so different from what you are used to. The further one goes on the spiritual path, the less definite one's self-perception becomes. You drop all of your accumulated "training" in how and who you are *supposed to be*, and instead become as innocent as an unspoiled child, totally authentic in each and every moment you experience.

We are telling you this so you will not think there is something wrong with you when your memory begins to go, when you have trouble remembering things that relate to time and past and future. You will be less inclined to make plans, because as soon as you do, you will find things have changed and you will very quickly realize the futility of trying to second-guess the next turn in the road. This is as it should be. You are simply shedding your conditioned responses and becoming more authentically who your soul wishes you to be.

Your body probably has had some strange feelings going off in it lately—a little like pings and pops in the most unlikely places, and with no apparent order or logic. You may have felt a surprising tenderness [soreness] in some places. You may run a fever or feel heat in some localized portion of your body. These are all signs of energetic patterns being cleared or corrected. Your "wiring" has been dysfunctional for quite a while. Now your circuits are being repaired and the life current is beginning to flow again. As it does, where there are "blockages" of stagnant energy, you will experience a temporary congestion, which is expressed as heat or mild pain. You may ease this process with finger pressure on the affected spots. You do not need to press hard. Just make firm contact with the spot and hold the intention that the energy blockage will dissolve and let the energy flow smoothly through that area. Use your intuition or your subtle senses to tell you when you are "done" with the spot. With practice, you can feel the energy begin to move, and then settle down into an even flow.

We have already spoken about the importance of meditation.

We cannot emphasize too strongly how important it is that you make the time and space for regular attempts at connecting with Source. Whether you are new to this or an "old hand," it is important to develop a strong habit of inner listening. Your life depends on it, in that you must be able to hear and respond to the inner promptings that speak ever so softly within you. We will give you more simple techniques for honing this ability as we go on, but for now we just wanted to let you know that this is more important in getting you to where you are supposed to go than anything else you could do.

In addition to meditation, it is important that you love and cherish yourself enough to make your spiritual practice the center of your life. Everything you do should support it. If it means creating a "sacred space" in your home, do that. Use pictures, objects, incense, candles, lighting, furniture, cloths—anything that will visually remind you that you are dedicating yourself to the attainment of your destiny. You will want to simplify your life if it is too crowded with activity, to clear the way for more "quiet time." Baths are good if you can use them to relax further, to become more receptive. Essential oils that make you feel relaxed and open are helpful. Anything that assists you in the redirection of your attention to what is going on inside of you will help. Turning off the TV will be a BIG help!!!

The reason we are speaking to you in this way at this time is to assist you in your transition from an ordinary "Earth human" back to the magnificent creature—a child of the Universe—that you are. All of these Messages have as their intention the redirection of your priorities to what is really important—those actions, thoughts, and intentions that are supportive of your return to full Mastery, for only Masters will occupy Terra. We will have more to say on that subject later.

As things "amp up" on the Earth plane, there will be much going on to distract you. There will be dramatic occurrences of all kinds. Your transition to Terra will go more smoothly if you can distance yourself from getting too caught up in the drama. Your media is the worst offender in the purveying of drama. Drama sells. In a world based on consumption rather than conservation, drama plays a big role in driving things forward in a downward direction. It will look and feel like everything is coming apart. It will look and CAN feel like you are at risk or in danger in some way, as the "chickens" lose their heads and go about shrieking that the sky is falling. You are not chickens. You are eagles. You will soar. While others are still pecking at the ground for crumbs, you will be taking your place at the banquet table. We are telling you this now, because soon your perceptual screen will be filled with scenes of drama. Detach from it. It is not what it appears.

Just as your body experiences strange localized clearings, the body of the Earth will be doing the same. It is all in Divine Order and as it should be. As the body of the Earth experiences localized clearings, the thoughtforms that were frozen there will be released. All of the human experience will be playing out before your eyes, a re-run of a different kind than your usual summer fare. Just remember to create your sanctuary within yourself and you will not be so inclined to get caught up in the hysteria. You must become calm in the midst of the storm, like the eye of a hurricane. No one can provide this for you. You can receive support for this, but you must be in your inner sanctuary to receive it. Let your physical senses see and hear what is going on around you if you wish, but withdraw your sense of "you" deeply within. Give yourself as much quiet time as you can. Listen, listen, listen inside. Tune out the noise of the rising chaos. Become quieter as things become louder. Wean yourself from the media of all kinds. Nothing "out there" has anything to offer but more chaos, more things to be afraid of. Even the "human interest" stories have at their core a feeling of estrangement from one another. They tend to view other people's lives like looking at germs under a microscope. They elevate the emotions to keep you caught up in the drama. Disconnect from that manipulation of your reality. Go inside for your "news of the day." You will find that your inner "station" is the one that tells you what you really need to know.

We shall speak to you again. For now, we leave you in peace and honor and blessing. Amen, Adonoy Sabayoth. We are the Hosts of Heaven.

5

A GUIDED TOUR OF TERRA
July 4, 1999

Today we would like to take you on a guided tour of Terra, so that you will have some idea of your destination and will then be able to relate better to the changes you are experiencing as you transform yourselves into those beings you will express as in the Terran landscape. We begin our tour from space, where we see Terra gleaming as a perfect blue pearl in the "sky" [of space]. She inspires love just to look at her. She gleams with an "unEarthly" light, as she is now glorified beyond your ability to imagine. To physical eyes, she would appear as a blue-white star, but to those eyes that can see at the finer levels of reality, she is radiant and welcoming to all those who operate on the frequencies of Love.

Extraordinary light streams from her, for at this stage she does not reflect light (as in her present state) but *radiates* it. (You will all be very radiant, too!) We hear a sound. It is exquisite—the "music of the spheres." It is the sound that every planet makes when it is totally harmonized with its place in the cosmos. To your present state of mind, it would sound truly "heavenly." When you are there, you will "live heaven"; your moment-to-moment experience will be that you are in "heaven," as it can be glimpsed through the shadows of your present state of awareness.

Drawing in closer now, we are struck by the fact that everything on the surface of the planet—its trees, animals, birds, fish in the oceans, but also the trees and flowers, even the air itself—is radiant with beauty, peace, and harmony. It is the crowning of Earth's own exploration of her theme of "seeking harmony in diversity." Every atom of this reality is in full consciousness, is fully aware of every other atom in that reality and consciously cooperating with the whole. It is like many voices merged into one glorious song.

To grasp an inkling of how pervasive this level of cooperation is, suppose that at some future moment, you would experience the desire for a piece of fruit from some particular tree that you will pass. That tree would put forth a blossom and form that fruit in such a way that it will be at its moment of perfect ripeness just as you pass by and put up your hand for it. (Actually, a measure of the same thing happens to you now, but there is so much "static" on the line, so to speak, that you are not aware of it. Everything always is and has been coordinated perfectly... but we digress.) On Terra, all IS the expression of unobstructed perfection. Everything is raised and glorified to its most exalted physical expression.

This is a physical world, or at least it is experienced that way. You will do the same types of things that you do now, but you will do them in a perfected way. You will still eat, make love, sleep, meditate, have pursuits that please you, but you will not be restricted by the constraints of an economic system that seeks only to take from you. In the perfected level of cooperation that exists on Terra, all parts support all the other parts. There is not poverty, disease, or dying in the sense that you now experience. When you eat a piece of fruit, it merges with you and becomes you, so it has not died; it has only changed form.

You will all be immortal beings. You will simply change form also, but you will do it without needing to "die and be reborn." You will be able to transition from one adult form to another. There will be children born on Terra. There will be families. But the children being born will be the projections of those souls whose third-density vehicles were shed and who "qualify" for fourth-density existence. Once they are "born" into fourth density, they need never "die" again. They will simply move on to other realms of experience and service. The rate of reproduction on Terra is precisely balanced with the harmony of the whole. Not one leaf, fruit, or child comes into that world that is not in keeping with the harmony of the whole. There is no excess; there is no lack. As expressed in your tale of Goldilocks [and the Three Bears], it will be "just right."

As we said in our last Message, you will operate from an inner knowing of what is "right." Terra will function as one giant organism, with each of the forms that exist on her functioning perfectly as part of that organism, just as the cells in a perfectly healthy body carry out their roles in harmony with the whole.

Some things will seem like they are simply higher versions, more perfected versions, of things you are already familiar with. People will still make love, for example, but no child will be conceived until it is the perfect moment for that to occur. You will be totally free to explore your sexual expression without fear of unwanted consequences. There is no death or disease on Terra, no need for protection from unwanted conditions. Everything proceeds in harmony with the whole. You are totally free to create whatever you wish, but you will only want to create in harmony with the whole.

Terra will be the garden spot of the galaxy, a living "school" in which the various cultures of the galaxy will be able to experience living in harmony with others who are very different from themselves. There will be distinct communities of every type of being that qualifies for Terran life. Each community will have its own ways, its own cultural predilections. One will be able to tour these different "villages" and experience the different cultural flavors that exist in the galaxy, and see how they can all relate to one another in harmony and peace.

Terra is the crown jewel of the galaxy, at least that portion of it that is functioning as fourth-density positive. There is a vibrational "barrier" at these higher levels that prevents any being or lifeform from entering the Terran space if that lifeform is not "qualified" by its own energy to do so. That is why you will not see disease-producing organisms there. They are the stuff of lower frequencies and are of the negative polarity expression, which has to do with entropy and death. Those who choose the negative polarity will have an abundance of death and disease, but they will have their own version of Earth to explore. Terra is not available to them.

So what will you do with yourselves? For one thing, you will travel a great deal. You will travel from one community to another, and to different spots in the galaxy that serve your further exploration and experience of life. You see, Terra will not have drama anymore. It will be very "tame," compared to your present experience. There will not be any mountains, as mountains occur only when there is tension and collision between the crustal plates. The present Earth has such monuments to the strains she has been put under, but on Terra, all of these will be smoothed out. The surface will be even and sculpted into the most beautiful gardens. Even the atmosphere will be in harmony. There will only be gentle rains—no thunderstorms. You may want to travel to other places to experience some of the excitement that such dramatic displays provide. You will be totally free to find whatever pleases you to experience, both on the planet and off of it.

We cannot speak in detail of your individual paths or experiences, because you are all unique and your explorations and preferences will be unique. We can only speak in general terms, as you will only discover the exact nature of your life as you live it. That will still be true at all levels of reality, as even the Creator likes to be surprised. That is why the Creator plays hide-and-seek with Itself through Its many forms. There is always a mystery unfolding, and one never reaches the end. The Creation is always birthing itself, so there is no end to the possible experiences that can be had. It is a lot like a fractal design. Each part of the fractal unfolds itself a little like a "twig off the old tree," but it does so in symmetry and perfection, and gives rise to other branches of itself that go on to do the same. That is how the Creator creates, like a fractal. It is the simplest expression that allows for all possibilities. Each point in the Creation is like a "seed" in a fractal. It becomes a site through which the Creator can unfold itself endlessly, creating new branches as it grows.

You are each one of those seed-points, and you are each a co-creator with the Creator, directly unfolding a particular exploration of reality from within you. We will have a discussion of how the different geometrical forms express this unfoldment at a later

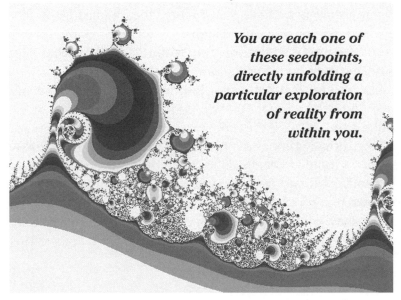

You are each one of these seedpoints, directly unfolding a particular exploration of reality from within you.

time. We mention these things now in order for you to have the proper context in which to place our words. In the end, you must experience it before you will "know" it, but we share these pictures with you now to give you a vision of "things to come" that you can hold in your hearts and minds and that will sustain you through the years of transition that lie directly ahead.

We will return to these thoughts in later Messages. Each Message will build upon the information of the previous Messages, unfurling in a perfect spiral. That is the shape of the evolutionary path. (The devolutionary path is a spiral, also, but instead of expanding infinitely, it compresses infinitely until at some point it must reverse course and begin expanding again or it will entirely disappear.) You are being lifted out of your mundane experience by your ability to respond to the incoming frequencies of Light. You built yourself to be able to do this at the appointed time. It is encoded in your cells, in your cellular memory. That is why you cannot "earn" your way onto Terra. You made the choice for that destination before you came into your present vehicle. If someone *appears* to be "missing the mark," or not "getting the message," consider the possibility that they are that way by their own soul's choice. There are no accidents. Everything is being coordinated from the highest levels of your being, but as we said before, the Creator loves to be surprised, so you will only discover what you "planned" to do as it unfolds from within you across time. (Time is what keeps everything from happening at once, you know.)

Life is a constantly unfolding journey, and that will not change when you get to Terra. You will continue to explore your own unique expression, but in conscious harmony with the whole. Your own creative impulses and curiosity will spur you on. You will neither be "bored to death" or numbed by perfection. Rather, you will finally be totally free to create, and what you create will be your own branch of the Creation.

We leave you now in peace and honor and blessing. We shall speak to you again. Amen, Adonoy Sabayoth. We are the Hosts of Heaven.

6

MERGING OF REALITIES
July 5, 1999

Today we will speak to you of some of the experiences you will be having as you journey back to full consciousness and your "homecoming." You are indeed now moving back to your true home, your true Self, and as these higher realities open to you, you will begin to have strange experiences that you can't explain to others. They will feel natural to you, but your social conditioning would label them as "strange," so you might begin to experience some fear around this issue. We have spoken of the necessity to move beyond fear into love, so we offer these comments today to reassure you that there is nothing to fear here. You are simply returning to the way you were before you took on these "garments" of flesh.

In the beginning, all was a sort of cosmic "soup." Everything was liquid and without defined form. Your scientists have approached this "soup" when they are able to create a plasma by using electromagnetic fields. It is a field or substrate of intelligent energy, but has no form of its own. Out of this intelligent "soup," all form emerged, self-aware to the extent that it knew it existed, but not able to reflect upon itself. That would appear later in the scheme of things.

In this soup, all things are contained in potential. You cannot see any of them, because they exist only as a potential—a possibility out of many possibilities. We mentioned fractals yesterday. If you think of a decision point—something simple like "What will I have for breakfast?"—you will be able to follow what we are talking about here. You can have many things for breakfast. You could use something that you already have in the house, you could go to the store and buy something else, or you could go to a restaurant and choose from their menu. Even breakfast offers a multitude of possibilities. These are decision points. They offer many possibilities, not just the two or three of "Yes," "No," or "Maybe." Each decision leads to other decision points. Let's say you decide to have eggs for breakfast, as part of your "breakfast" decision. Now you are faced with other decision points: How will you make your eggs? Scrambled? Poached? Fried? Boiled? And the from THAT decision, you will have other decisions to make. What will you have with your eggs? What "goes" with the eggs depends in part on how you decided to prepare the eggs. Scrambled eggs might call for the addition of some milk or onion. Boiled eggs might call for some mayonnaise or salt and pepper.

We use this simple example to show you how one set of possible decisions leads to other possible decisions. Computer programmers would call these "logic branches." You can go this way (scrambled) or this way (poached) or this way (boiled), and so on. Then once one has chosen to travel through one "gate" to the exclusion of the other ones, other "branches" present. In a fractal design, one can see this represented graphically. The origin point produces branches infinitely, as long as the values stay within certain limits. One can "explore" fractals endlessly as long as one stays within those limits. This is the way the Creation unfolds itself from within that cosmic "soup." It begins to branch immediately by expressing a "set" of possibilities or potentials. Every time a "decision" is made to choose one possibility over the others, that decision point or branch becomes the starting place for a new set of possibilities, as we showed in the breakfast example. But that's how the whole thing began—with a set of possibilities—so we have just recapitulated the starting point. This is called an "iteration." An iteration is a cycle through a certain formula. Mathematicians use iterations to solve complex equations.

So this is how the Creation unfurls—through a series of iterations (cycles) of a complex formula that allows for an infinite number of decision points or branches to be explored. But what of the other points or branches? Well, the Creator explores them, too. But how can you have both poached eggs and fried eggs and boiled eggs and scrambled eggs? You probably wouldn't want to have all of them at the same time. The Creator solves this dilemma by creating separate realities to accommodate all of the possible choices. If one expression of "you" chooses the poached eggs, there will be other expressions of "you" to make the other choices, and they will all go on, branching and branching and branching…

If you look at the fractal design at the bottom of this page, you will see what we are talking about. This is how the Creation unfolds. Each branch leads to other branches. There are as many realities as there are points of awareness to experience them. There are as many expressions of "you" as are required to explore all the possibilities. You are an expression of the Creator. You could say you ARE the Creator-in-expression. The Creator (being THE Creator), wants to experience (or "explore") ALL of the branches, which are

essentially infinite in number, within certain limits or parameters. Those limits we call "Universal Laws." They are not like the laws that are passed by your governments. They apply to all created realities, on all levels of being. There are subsets of these laws that apply to specific frequency bands (densities or "dimensions" as some people call them—density is the more correct term), but the truly "universal" laws apply to all of Creation. Your scientists are forever searching for the theories that unify other theories into a simpler, more inclusive whole. Universal laws are the reduction of all subsets of "rules" to the Grand Unified Law (or blueprint) for all of Creation. They are encoded in all of material matter and can be accessed by a properly attuned mind.

You—as you currently experience yourself—appear to be a "bag of skin." But there is so much more to you than that. The real "you" is expressing simultaneously on all the logic branches that arose as potentials when your soul was created, or "split off" from the Creator's identification with Itself. Your soul is a projection of the Creator. It IS the Creator, as it contains all aspects of the Creator, but it also experiences itself as slightly different from the Creator. It is a more individuated or "specialized" aspect of the Creator. It is an "expert" or "specialist" in certain themes, which are sometimes called archetypes. However, even within this individuation, there are an infinite number of potentials to be explored, within the parameters of Universal Laws. So you all have been quite busy at the soul level, creating many parallel versions of "lives," through which you can explore many realities. In fact, you gave yourselves billions of years in which to explore those realities, but now that cycle is coming to an end. It is almost time to hit the "refresh" button on the Creation, to clear out all the fragments on the experiential screen that are left over from previous experiments—to re-draw the creation anew [just as the Refresh button on your Web browser re-loads and re-draws the page you are looking at].

We shall leave the discussion of the cycles involved for another time. For now, just know that all the explorations available within this "set" of possibilities have been nearly exhausted; it is nearly time to bring those "lives" to an end and to close the "set" so another one can be used to replace it. In your theatrical productions, you "strike the set" when the drama is over, when the play closes down. It is just that way on the "stage" now. The "set" will close down and be replaced by another. This means that all of the parallel realities that you have been exploring will terminate and be replaced by a new insertion point into a whole other "set" of possibilities. There is always a single "seed" point that marks the beginning of some process. There is also a logical end point to the process. You have called these the "Alpha" (beginning) and the "Omega" (end). You are nearly at the Omega Point and will soon experience a new Alpha pPoint. In between, there is a Null Point in which nothing exists.

You may be surprised to know that you don't exist all of the time now. You are actually blinking on and off many times a second. Your movies are made up of discrete snapshots, or "frames," none of which are "moving," but when they are projected onto a screen in your movie theaters, they flash on and off so fast that the retention of the image [from one frame to the next] makes them appear to be moving smoothly and without interruption. Those people who make animations for the Web know that their animations actually contain several different "frames" or still pictures that appear to move when exhibited on the screen for an appropriately short period of time. Your reality, which appears to you to be continuous and solid, is actually made up of static images—holograms—which flash on and off several times a second, quickly enough that you don't perceive the "off" times but instead experience a "continuous" reality. It is anything but continuous, so the Null Point that we mention is nothing "new," but it IS significant because of what it represents.

Instead of a simple movement from one frame to another—say your head nods downward a tiny fraction of an inch and your hand moves upward a similarly small increment toward your nose, which has started to itch—this Null Point will be what is called a "quantum moment," a gigantic leap onto a whole other experience of reality. The Creation will literally come to an end and be RE-created in the next "frame." It will be re-seeded with a whole new "set" of possibilities. In the moment in between the Omega Point and the Alpha Point, there will literally be "no thing"—there will be no manifest reality anywhere. There will only be the Creator, in a perfect state of rest, but containing all things in potential.

The "you" that you experience now is really only a point of awareness within the All That Is, the expressed portion of the Creator. There are an infinite number of such points, according to the branches that have been explored. But there is only going to be ONE "you"—the "seed" of the new "set" that is about to be created on the other side of the Omega Point. So what happens to all the other "you"s that have been out there exploring all the other realities? They will be folded back into your soul and merged with it, just as happens each and every time a "life" is ended. But the "you" that is reading this [Message] is the one that is going to "go across" into the new reality, so you will begin "seeing" through the eyes of your soul. You will begin to see more and more of the other realities that these other portions or aspects of "you" have been exploring. From the perspective of the "you" that is reading this Message, it will seem as though those other realities are "merging with" or "coming into" your own.

There is nothing in your mass culture or literature to explain this to you. That is one of the reasons that we are giving this series of Messages to you, to explain to you what is happening now, and to reassure you that you are not "going crazy." You remember we told you to become aware of your breath? Notice what your breath is doing now. Take a deep breath now. Feel the difference.

This information is bound to set up a "but, but, but" response from the level of your ego or personality. It will protest mightily against the magnitude of what we are saying here. Your ego is designed to keep "body and soul" together, so if it hears that it is going to "end," that causes the ego to clamp down into "protection mode," which is experienced as fear. The breath shortens and becomes shallow, as all systems go on "red alert" until the perceived danger is identified and assessed. When you become aware of your breath being short and shallow, *will* yourself to take a deep breath and give your body and ego the message that you are safe. This is very important. You must begin to develop your own ability to create a sense of safety for yourself, because otherwise you will react from a place of fear—from your ego rather than your higher knowing—and make bad decisions. You will not respond appropriately to the changes that present to you as this cycle of Creation completes.

The parallel realities will merge. They have been doing so gradually for some time now, but now this process will accelerate. This is all leading to the Omega Point and the crossing through the Null Point into the Alpha Point. It is all being sourced and guided from the higher levels, and you do not have to "figure it out." You are passengers on this trip, not the pilot. Breathe. Meditate. Accept. Relax into it. You are on the most wonderful "magical mystery tour" of all time! Enjoy it. Become like a little child in front of a big department store, peering in through the plate glass window at all the wonders inside. Develop your sense of wonder. Allow your mental "analyst" to take a rest. Just relax, breathe, and sink into this experience of multiple realities. It is part of your preparation to accept the "new you," that multidimensional being that will emerge on the other side of the Null Point.

This is why we have told you to give your spiritual practice the highest importance now. It is of the utmost value at this time to create as much "quiet time" as you can. You will need it to calm yourself, to integrate the many new experiences and insights that begin to flood into you as your Light fibers are reconnected. A great deal of your transformation will take place now, on this side of the Null Point. All of these separate "you"s will be merged with your soul, and you will begin to access their awareness and experience. Your apparently solid reality will appear to be melting and you will begin to exist more and more in an "altered state" of consciousness. You will need these periods of quiet to integrate all of this. It is no small thing that is happening here, and we want you to know that there is a tremendous amount of support that is available from the higher realms, but we cannot give it unless you ask for our assistance. We cannot infringe on your free will. In the chatter of ego mind, there is a lot of "static" on the line, a lot of churning of emotions, all of which obscure and distort the "still, small voice" within you. You need these quiet times to be able hear us and feel us. You need to give this to yourself if you wish to have as smooth a transition as possible.

In closing, we wish to assure you that—outside of time—you have already gotten "there." You will not "miss the boat." You cannot "blow it." Your soul will guide you perfectly. But you will have a much easier time of it if you can follow our suggestions and relax, breathe, meditate, and simplify your lives so you have more and more quiet time. We leave you now in peace and honor and blessing. Amen, Adonoy Sabayoth. We are the Hosts of Heaven.

7

THE HARVESTING OF SOULS
July 6, 1999

Today we shall be introducing a new idea or concept—the existence of multiple "selves" all at the same time. If you were to look at reality from the perspective of the Oversoul, you would see all of your "lives" going on simultaneously. You would see that you had created them and you would have very little interest in what was happening to them because you created them WHOLE, i.e. containing everything they needed to complete the life "design" you intended for them. It is a little like the "oak tree inside the acorn" analogy. When a "life" is created, it contains "codings"—very similar to computer programs and subprograms—that will unfold the life perfectly. These codings are contained in the DNA and the various parts of the cells and tissues that make up the body. They are only contained in the brain to the extent that they exist in the cells of the brain. The brain does not "think" or direct. It is merely a switching station that coordinates signals or information exchange between the many different parts of the body and interprets the data coming in from the sensory input mechanisms.

Each "life" is actually a projection of the Oversoul into a particular space/time environment. It is connected to the Oversoul by the "silver cord," a filament that directly connects the physical body to the Oversoul and which acts as a communication link between the Oversoul and the body or "life." The Oversoul exists outside of linear time, and so from its perspective, all of its projections are going on simultaneously. It is free to terminate a life, in which case it simply disconnects the silver cord, or create one, in which case it extends a silver cord into a developing fetus. Time is a vector quantity, associated with material reality. Since the Oversoul exists in non-material reality, it is outside of linear time.

Time is a way of defining location. For example, if you say you were born in Baton Rouge, you must also say WHEN you were born, in order to precisely locate the event. You could understand this by imagining a street on which a parade was going to pass. The parade streams through that street at a particular time. If you were in that parade playing the drum, you could locate yourself by saying, "I will pass by the corner of Main and Oak Streets at precisely 11:11 a.m. on Tuesday, July 6, 1999." That way, not only could you place yourself within time, but so could any other event that needed to intersect with you, according to ITS plan for itself. Time not only keeps things from happening all at once, it also provides the necessary component for things to move or progress.

So, to return to the Oversoul, from outside of time—which is where the Oversoul resides—all of its projections are simultaneous. But from within time, each life is experienced as being separated across time. You speak of "past lives" and sometimes "future lives," but those are expressions of the experience of being bound by linear time. You can "remember" these other "lives" by accessing the information in the Oversoul. The Oversoul is the repository of all the personal memories, from all of the "lives" it creates. When it is appropriate, one of your subprograms kicks in and you "remember" something from these other "lives," to assist you in unfolding your "program" for the "life" you experience yourself as living.

There is no such thing as "re"-incarnation. There is only "incarnation." The Oversoul projects itself into a space/time locus and clothes the tip of that projection in a "body." It is like putting a finger in a bowl of pudding. The finger is part of you. The pudding represents the space/time environment into which you put your finger. The fingertip can feel the pudding. It can tell if it is warm or cold, soft, wet, dry, or firm. Just so with you. You are the sensory tip of a "finger" of your Oversoul, thrust into the "pudding" of your present space/time environment. You interact with your environment, which includes the presence of "fingers" from other Oversouls, each sensing and interacting with the same environment, but from their own perspective. The experience of reality is totally SUBJECTIVE. There is no "objective" reality that everyone can agree upon, because each point of awareness has its own perspective, and sees things from a slightly different "angle." That is how the Creator gets to view Itself from all possible "angles" at once.

We are using the term Oversoul today, but in past Messages we have referred to it as the soul, because that is a more familiar term to most of you. Each of these Messages is building upon the ones that have gone before, in a spiral fashion. Each Message builds upon the previous ones and lays the groundwork for the following ones. This is the way the Universe unfolds itself. The "soul" is actually like a bead on the silver cord, between the Oversoul and the "body" of the life. It is like a local supervisor and only has that one "life" to contend with. Its job is to closely monitor and interact with that "life" and to assist it in fulfilling its purpose in being. When the silver cord is withdrawn by the Oversoul, the soul is pulled back up into the Oversoul and merges into it. All of the experiences of the "life" flow up the silver cord during that life, so the soul does not contain anything other than its capacity to assist that life in fulfilling its purposes.

Now that all but one of the "lives" are being terminated, the Oversoul is "harvesting" its accumulated experience and preparing to make a quantum leap into another reality. Even Oversouls "graduate" and move up the evolutionary ladder, back to Source. In reality, Source IS everything all at once, but from the subjective perspective of any individuated portion of the Absolute, it has its awareness placed somewhere along the evolutionary flow that proceeds forth from Source (the Absolute) and back into Source, continuously, like an unending river or stream of consciousness that has no beginning or end.

However, sometimes—across very long periods of time as you

know it—Source "blinks" or "swallows." You are approaching one such event. The Oversouls are individuated portions of Source, and they are all in direct communication with Source. You might liken them to the "fingers" of Source, as in our pudding example above. They are an intermediate step between "All There Is" and the individual "lives" being lived. (As we have said, there is only ONE LIFE being lived, through its many expressions. That is why we have been placing quotation marks around the word "life" or "lives." They are "relative," and subjective. Only the Absolute—Source—is absolute and objective. This will have significance later on, when we discuss holograms.)

Source is going to "blink" soon, and on the other side of the blink It will "see" a very different Creation. This is not provided for in any of the cosmologies you have available, which is why we are providing this information now—to help you understand what is about to happen and the magnitude of it. In virtually all cosmologies, you have made the assumption that life proceeds in cycles of symmetric or logarithmic shape. You assume that if it took so many billions of years to reach a certain evolutionary state, that it will take a similar amount of time to complete the "return" trip. In the models of the "ages," you have two kinds: those in which the "ages" are of the same length (such as the Piscean Age or the Age of Aquarius), and those in which the "ages" have a logarithmic relationship to each other (such as in the "yugas" and the traditions that refer to very long "golden" ages, followed by shorter "silver" ages, followed by still shorter ages, until you get to the one you are experiencing now, the shortest and most difficult of all). Those systems propose that the next step after the shortest age is another "golden" age—from shortest age to longest age in one step, which is closer to what will be happening now.

However, there is a significant difference this time. In a message that was delivered through J. J. Hurtak some years ago, reference is made to the "respatialization of consciousness" following the Null Point (he called it the Gravity Null Zone). This is very accurate. The Creation is about to be entirely re-created. All the foci of consciousness will be "blinked off" for an immeasurable "moment." (Time will also cease, as there will be no material reality in that moment and time is a function of material reality; it is the "time" portion of space/time.) On the other side of the "blink," the "players" in the drama of Creation will find themselves standing on other "spots" on the "stage." It will be like closing your eyes and then reopening them, only to find that the scene you are looking at has changed drastically.

What this means is that all of the stuff of prediction is rendered null and void. All of the human prophets and seers have seen through the perspective of the present reality. There is no one that is or was in a physical body that can accurately predict what is about to happen or what one will experience after that "blink" has occurred. Each and every Oversoul will be affected in ways that even the Oversouls cannot anticipate. Their only task is to prepare themselves for the event by completing all of their "lives," harvesting all but one of the souls back into the Oversoul, and retaining one portion of exteriorized consciousness with which to "seed" the new Creation. There will be many fewer players on the "stage" when the new drama unfolds. You who are reading this Message will be among those who are there to experience it, but you will be much changed from your present form and identity. You are being prepared by your Oversoul and overseen by your soul for this event. We are doing our best to prepare you so that you will not be overwhelmed by the magnitude of what is happening and by the new sensations and awarenesses that have begun to enter your consciousness.

Many of you naturally have come to revere the great beings who have appeared on the world stage—the Christ, the Buddha, and others. Now YOU will become as they were. You have another job ahead, and in order to step into those "shoes" and fill them, you must step out of the ones you are wearing now.

This is the time of the harvest of the souls. Everyone who is in a body has a soul. This is the time of the great "summing up" of all of the "lives" lived. Depending on the "total," each Oversoul will come to its own conclusions about what it wishes to create next. There is no damnation, no "judgement" by a wrathful God. (It should really be spelled with a little "g," for the Absolute is the absolute, and "wrath" is a human projection onto the Absolute that is entirely misplaced. There HAVE been entities that have appeared as "gods" in their interaction with humankind on Earth, but that is another story for another time.) But here is where it gets interesting for you: you are the one "life" that will be retained to seed the new Creation. You have great adventures ahead of you, and you have begun your transformation into that being that you will experience yourself as being on the other side of the "blink." All is in hand. All is being prepared. You have suffered enough, beloveds. Soon you will be at the banquet, with all of your fellow Wanderers. You will have much fun in creating something entirely new.

Enjoy yourselves in these remaining days. Do not worry about the scare tactics of the various entities who have a different idea of how it will go. They will not be around in your reality on the other side of the "blink." Everything has its place in the Creation. You have yours; they have theirs. We are assisting in these matters to make sure that everyone gets to their own "right place." No longer will it be necessary for Earth to host such contention and division. She will be able to pursue her theme of "seeking harmony in diversity," but now it will be as it was originally intended—a diversity of forms and cultures, all of whom will be resonant with the new vibratory frequency that will characterize the New Earth, Terra. These contentious ones will have their own world in which to continue their battles with each other. They will not bother you anymore, and they will finally be free of you and your reminders of what they are not. Everyone will end up at home in the vibratory band that is most akin to his or her nature.

You—because you have read this far—are destined for Terra. If you were not, you would have left off reading these Messages awhile back. They are coded transmissions, and you will only respond favorably to them if you carry the matching coding within you. You are small in number relative to the total population of Earth—less than 1/10 of 1%. But you are the seeds for the new garden, the new birth of Earth in her glorious time as Terra.

Happy journey! We shall speak to you again. Amen, Adonoy Sabayoth. We are the Hosts of Heaven.

"All natures, all formations, all creatures exist in and with one another, and they will be resolved again into their own roots. For the nature of matter is resolved into the roots of its nature alone. He who has ears to hear, let him hear."
—The Gnostic Gospel of Mary [Magdalene]

8

ON PROBABILITIES
July 7, 1999

In today's Message, we want to speak about probabilities. You know how many are going about these days proclaiming that they know what is going to happen, that it will be such and such, and they are very sure that it will be as they say. However, NO ONE knows what is really going to happen, not even us, because there are only indications of what will "probably be" the case. We can say, with a reasonable degree of certainty, that such and such will *probably* be the outcome of certain observed trends, but no one can really be certain. The Creator is playing hide-and-seek with Itself and apparently even It likes to be surprised. It's what keeps the game interesting. If one could predict with absolute certainty everything that would happen, one would scarcely have to "get up in the morning." It would make for a very dull existence, indeed.

The whole reason the Creation was created was so that the Creator could experiment with ALL of the different possibilities (within certain parameters, called Universal Laws), so It could get to hide from Itself and so discover Itself in an unending mystery unfolding. The Creator "likes" to be surprised, because the reality game is Its only entertainment. Think about it: here you are, All That Is. Everything is contained within you, and you are everywhere at once. There is no place to "go" because you are already "there." So what do you do for entertainment? You surprise yourself.

(You are a "chip off the old block," so to speak—a projection from an individuated portion of the Creator—so you show glimpses of the Creator's nature. It is not so "off" to project "human" traits onto the Creator, because one can glimpse the Creator through Its creations. The true human is the crown of material reality; it comes the closest to the nature of the Creator, so we can get some idea of what "makes the Creator tick" by observing true humans.

You (in your present state) are not true humans, as we have said, but hybrids. In the transformation you are undergoing right now, you will be returning to your true human status. Viewed from your present state of affairs, you will be as "gods," but that is our point. Even though you are not yet returned to your fully conscious state, you still have enough of the human quality in you to glimpse what you will be like in your fully conscious state. And from that, you can impute what the Creator is like, and can attribute human qualities to the Creator.)

So, the Creator likes surprises. It always has something up Its sleeve, so to speak. And here we are, sailing along in a particular direction, expecting such and such to happen, and then Wham! Out of the blue. A surprise. It could not be anticipated, not even by us. Something or someone shows up that was wholly unplanned for, and it spins things into a totally unexpected direction. However, for a surprise to *really* be a surprise, you cannot even see an inkling of it coming. Those are the ones the Creator REALLY likes! Here we are, going along, doing our best to carry out our service, trying to anticipate what we will have to prepare for, and then Boom! Along comes a surprise and it's back to the drawing boards. And if WE—given the level we operate at—can't make solid plans and expect them to last, just imagine how unclear the picture is for those in your state of consciousness who claim to "know" the future! That's why you never find anyone "batting 1000." No channel, no seer, no prophet of any shape or size, can know the future with any degree of certainty. And this is both a source of frustration and a great comfort at the same time.

We have spoken of the need to trust in the Creator, as a component of our definition of love. We have to trust in the Creator, too. Now we get to the heart of the matter. In these most uncertain of times, there are many things that are hidden from us as well as you. All we—or anyone—can do is try to put our efforts behind the most likely outcomes and try to take advantage of the momentum in that direction. We are dealing with a set of probabilities, i.e. that there is a certain degree of likelihood that such and such will happen. We put all of our best efforts into trying to maximize that potential in a direction that would please us, but as you know from your own lives, sometimes things change.

We began the preparation for the transition to Terra many centuries ago, as counted within your years. We had high hopes of a huge harvest for Terra. The probability was—say 80%—that that might be the case, so we threw all of our best efforts into sowing seeds that would make it possible to happen. But as you know from the story about casting seeds, some do not fall on good soil. Some begin to grow, but encounter conditions that do not allow them to finish growing. We are not omniscient, so we could not know in advance how all the Oversouls would play the game. No one was showing their cards to anyone else. It's made to be that way, for the reasons that we stated earlier.

Now, however, we are at the "end game" stage. There are certain geometries that occur in the movements of the planets, stars, galaxies, and indeed the entire system of created universes. They each have their own period, much like the gears in a clock-works. Each turns at different rates, and every so often, they align with other gears (planets, stars, and galaxies) in particular geom-etries that make certain potentials available. There is a "window of opportunity" available that permits or supports certain things that cannot occur at any other time. This is what is behind the system of divination you call astrology. When certain aspects or align-ments occur, it has been noticed that certain other phenomena are associated with them. This is true, because the "working beam" (holographic terminology) is altered in its orientation to the "reference beam" (the Absolute) so that a different "picture" (outpicturing) occurs in the hologram that constitutes your perceived reality. We shall have more to say on the subject of holograms later. The point of this is that if you picture all the "gears" to have a mark on them and that all the marks were lined up at the "beginning" of the Creation, they are all approaching that same alignment again. It is a window of opportunity for a new beginning, a wholly new Creation.

We have known that this opportunity was coming, and we wished to assist in ways that would maximize the harvest for Terra. There are other destinations for those who will not be going to Terra, but Terra is our "project," you might say, and that is where we put our energy. We knew that there was a great deal of inertia to overcome, due to the workings of the interlopers, but we put our shoulders to the wheel, so to speak, and put everything we had to work with toward the aim of maximizing the harvest for Terra. We knew the greatest probability was that the harvest would be small, so we put our efforts into that "marginal" area—toward reaching as many as possible who were on the margins—to try to get as many as we could to go over the line and make the grade, so to speak, who would not otherwise do so without our help.

You may have noticed that there were many predictions for Earth changes and such that simply did not manifest. Even now, the world has become a little more violent, the weather is definitely not "as usual," but little else seems to have changed. Things seem pretty much "business as usual." But there is this clockworks to contend with. Events cannot be delayed indefinitely. The Earth changes are a necessary part of the planet's preparation to become manifest as Terra. They are the way she will rid herself of the negativity and confusion that she has absorbed from human inter-ference with natural systems. We are approaching the end of the runway. We must now take flight, or never get off the ground. We have held back the Earth changes as long as we could so that we could put all of our efforts into reaching those who were marginal, who wouldn't make it to Terra without our help.

It is one minute to midnight. Soon all the gears will line up and a powerful beam of energy will manifest, all the way back to the Source. When this happens, there is this opportunity to re-create the Creation. It only occurs once in several billion years, so it is too rare and too precious an opportunity to waste. You are already within the influence of this beam, and the changes have begun. As you move through time toward the point of perfect alignment, the effects of this beam will grow and the pace of change will quicken until it is at a maximum. That is when the "leap" will occur. When that moment is reached, the Null Point will occur, and all the players will be rearranged into new configurations. The players include the planets and stars, because they are also conscious beings with destinies of their own. Earth will become Terra, and will operate at a different frequency band than she currently operates at. The Earth changes have to occur so that she is ready to make her leap when the moment presents. She cannot be weighed down by the "baggage" she has taken on from her human occupants. She has to shed all of it in order to be ready.

You, too—at least those of you who are destined for Terra—have been shedding your "baggage." You, too, cannot be weighed down, so that you are ready to make your leap into the next frequency band. Your "earthquakes" have been going on for some time now, only they have taken the form of shaking you loose from all of your activities and associations and relationships that did not serve your movement to Terra. We will be taking you to another place to complete your transition, so that you are ready to repopulate the Earth when she has completed her transition to becoming Terra. We will be doing this in stages. The first group is extremely small—only a handful—and will not be noticed except by those immediately involved with them. The second group will be fairly substantial, and the third group will be the largest of all and be taken at the last possible moment. The first two groups will be further along in their preparations by then, and will be involved in assisting those in the third group to adapt to their changing status.

As we have indicated, the harvest for Terra is less than 1/10 of 1% of the present world population. As small as that is, it would have been even smaller if we had not chosen to play the "probability" game. We are somewhat sad that we were not more successful, but we are gladdened by the success that we have achieved. More people "made the grade" than would have if we had not helped, and we are content with that. We did our best, and we, too, have to surrender to the higher authority. We, too, have to ACCEPT what has happened and how the "mop flopped."

Very soon, now, the first group will be taken. They know who they are and have been given clear guidance or at least a clear sense of their life winding up. We are giving these Messages now, so that they can remain available to those who will follow. By the way, some people who will be in the third group are there because they asked to be allowed to stay until the end so they could help for as long as possible. They are truly "saints" for that service, for it will be very demanding as the Earth changes begin in earnest and so many will need assistance. But they will have assistance by then, as those who "went" in the first group will be able to come back and assist in ways that they could not if they were still "mere mortals." We shall come back to this topic later.

For now, all you need to know is that the game is almost over. Things are going to get going, "big time," very soon, and we wanted to give you these Messages so you would be able to understand the larger picture that is unfolding behind the surface phenomena. We will have a few more Messages for you and then it will all be said. Then it will be up to you to take this information and put it to use, to keep it in your hearts and minds, to hold the shining promise of Terra before you as a vision of the horizon toward which you walk. It hopefully will sustain you as the world around you comes tumbling down and the doorway to your future swings open.

We leave you now in peace and honor and blessing. Amen, Adonoy Sabayoth. We are the Hosts of Heaven.

9

CHANGING INTO "GODS"

July 8, 1999

Today's Message will deal with holograms. Holograms form the basis of your perceived reality. The "you" that is reading this message is really a holographic projection of your Oversoul. You feel and look totally solid, but in fact that is part of the illusion of material reality. Without getting too technical, you are the result of interference patterns that result in standing waves. You are a package of standing waves.

Your physical body is contained in a matrix of Light. This Light is a substance, similar to water vapor, but much finer. It is incandescent, self-luminous, and so is often referred to as the Light Body. It is a matrix of Light in which the denser material that makes up the gross physical level is suspended, like so many particles in a soup. To "call down the Light Body" is ridiculous, as you would not be able to walk around if you weren't already "in" your Light Body. It is what shapes you, carries you, and forms you. It is the "template" for your form. It is the projection of your Oversoul, and without it, you simply would not exist in material reality. You are a hologram of Light, formed by Light. All holograms are formed by light, of one kind or another. You are made up of Light.

Each particle of matter is a densification of this Light. Each material object is floating in a sea of this Light. You can't see it with your physical eyes, but for those people who can see into the finer regions of reality, they are very aware of this. Why do we mention this? Because very soon now, you will be changing your form to more nearly resemble the perfected model of your Light Body.

We have mentioned the interlopers. They tinkered with the original design for the Adamic model and crossbred it with the higher apes on your planet. This led to some contamination of the encodings and the subsequent confusion of identity that resulted. You are going through a purification process that will enable you to shed all of the "impurities" of this hybridization, and will regain your natural form. To you, these forms will look so perfect that you would call yourselves "gods" (and "goddesses").

But there is more to this change than "meets the eye." To function on the next level of being, you must also have a change in your consciousness. We are gradually helping you to shift your identity, but we are also helping you to reconnect your unused Light circuitry, so that you will become fully conscious again. This is your true estate, your true nature, and we are here to help you regain your true station in the Creator's realm.

This shift will bring you many things. You will have all your powers back—the ability to create directly from the matrix of reality, the ability to move backward and forward through time, the ability to perform what you would call "miracles." You will have total Mastery, with all the "perks" that go with that, but you will also have the responsibility that goes with those "perks." You will not have powers that you do not also have the wisdom to use properly.

In order for you to have an environment that allows for the smooth transition to this "new you," we will be working with you to take you far enough to handle another vibratory level, and then you will simply vanish from the third-density plane and appear in the fourth-density plane, where we have prepared a place for you. You will reside there until Terra is ready for you and you are ready for Terra. For those that go in the first two waves, you will have work to do before Terra is ready. You will know more when you get there. All you need to know right now is that this will happen. These Messages are simply to prepare you for the change, not to describe every last detail of what will play out after that.

So this is a shift in frequency and it is also a shift in consciousness. You will find that you quite naturally begin functioning in new ways. Time and memory are the first things to go, but your bodies will also begin to operate differently. Pay attention to your bodies and what they are telling you. You may find that some foods no longer appeal to you and others suddenly become attractive. There are no rules to this game. You must throw out every idea of what you think is "how it is." Stay in the moment and "go with the flow." Surrender will be helpful in this. Just keep letting go and letting God, and you will have a much easier time of it. Wherever you cling to old ways, in whatever form, the pressure will build up until that grip is broken, for you cannot take any of the old ways into the new world. You are being re-created *in situ*. You will emerge as a fully formed, mature adult, without going through death, rebirth, and maturation. From one adult form to another.

So how do you accomplish this? You ACCEPT it. You focus on listening within and allowing the process to unfold within you. You allow yourself to melt and flow with the process. Resistance will be the source of all and any discomfort you may have with this process. Simply let go. If you find yourself in some form of discomfort, then do what you must to relax into it and it will shift. Take a bath. Meditate. Write your feelings. Breathe. Breathe. Breathe. Your breath is always a clue to whether you are holding onto something or letting go. Sigh a lot. That will give your body the message to keep on letting go. That feeling you have when you sigh—of emphasizing the exhale—is the body's way of saying it's letting go. Let go and let God. This should be your motto. This will help you more than anything else to get through this transition with the least discomfort possible. Everything of your old life is going to go, so why hang onto it? Just let go.

There is really not much more for us to say to you today, as letting go is the way through. All the mechanics and logistics are being handled for you, so just take a passenger seat and enjoy the view. You have not much longer to wait. Amen, Adonoy Sabayoth. We are the Hosts of Heaven.

10

ON EXTRATERRESTRIALS
AND THE HARVEST
July 9, 1999

Good day. Today we are going to touch on a very controversial subject—that of extraterrestrials, UFOs, and other such "fringe" phenomena. First of all, to define the word "extraterrestrial."

"Extra," used in this sense, means "outside of"; "terrestrial" means "having to do with the (planet) Earth." Please note that the word terrestrial contains the signature of Terra as the planet's true name. You are already on Terra, but not as she will become.

So extraterrestrial means "from outside of the planet Earth (Terra)." Well, you are ALL extraterrestrials in that sense, because you all are being projected from a level that is not based on the planet, and your bodies are made up of the elements that are the stuff of stars. You are truly *celestial* beings. Also note that the word "extraterrestrial" places Earth at the center of the universe and identifies everything that is not ON the Earth as being extra-terrestrial, a form of "us" and "them" thinking that is now obsolete. We prefer the term "celestials," but for this discussion, we will use your convention and refer to beings whose home base is not on the planet Earth as ETs.

ETs come in many shapes, sizes and forms. Your media has popularized the "little grey men" of Roswell fame, and the T-shirts and various "tourist" items are more often than not emblazoned with little slanty-eyed grey ETs. However sensational they are, and with them the tales of abductions, cattle mutilations, and sexual interchange, they are not all there is to this picture.

There are many races interacting with your people right now. The most visible are the ones who are in the lower frequency bands, but there are also ones that operate in the higher frequency bands. They are only visible to you in your "inner" vision. We are in this latter category for now. We do not usually materialize in the physical band, although we can if we choose to. We are in the bands that contain those you would call Masters, angels, and archangels. We work with the Office of the Christ. (That is not a particular person, but an office or position within the spiritual hierarchy.)

We [the ETs] come in two "flavors," according to our alignment and methods of operation (M.O.). We either serve others ("service to others," also known as STO) or we serve ourselves ("service to self," also known as STS). No matter what our particular form— our apparent "planet of origin"—that is the most important thing for you to know about us. Are we STS or STO? That M.O. defines how we will interact with you and what our true motives are. STS always want something from you that serves their own agenda, but is not in your best interests. STO is there to be of assistance in whatever way does not infringe upon your free will and choice. No matter how sweet the words are, it is always useful in dealing with those who are of a culture foreign to your own ("alien" means "foreign") to ask yourselves, "Who does this (action) serve? Is it in my best interests or theirs?"

Now, as we have said, there is ONLY ONE LIFE being lived. No matter what the current "costume" is, or the apparent behavior, it is all an expression of that one life, which you may call God, the Creator, Source, or All That Is. All ETs are expressions of that one life. We are not wanting to get into "us" and "them" thinking, "enemies" and "friends" divisions, but rather to take two steps back and simply observe: Who is served?

Now that we have laid the groundwork and vocabulary, we will say that we are of the STO variety of ET. We are here to help you in any way that we can that will not infringe on your own free choice. The interlopers of whom we have spoken are of the other "flavor." They are STS in their M.O., and as such they are not bound by such constraints. They can and will infringe on your choice in any way that you LET them, but they cannot override your free will. If you do not want to deal with them, all you need to do is to assert your free will. Tell them to leave and they must obey. Wherever you carry fear, that is a weak point, a place where you are vulnerable, and they operate best by playing on your fears. This is always the case. If you feel helpless or afraid in some way, they have gained power over you, and gaining power is their whole game. They literally feed off of it. You have observed some of this kind of behavior among certain people on Earth. It is of the same "flavor," no matter where you find it. Always ask, "Who does it serve?"

We have spoken of the harvesting of souls and the different "destinations" that will be available after the Null Point. Where one ends up is dependent on the sum of the choices that have been made by the souls belonging to a particular Oversoul. There will be a certain "Light quotient" contained within the Oversoul after it has harvested all of the souls that belong to it and absorbed them. This Light quotient determines the level at which the Oversoul vibrates, or its frequency. You might be surprised to find out that Oversouls come in two flavors, as well. Both flavors exist because the Creator wanted to experience EVERYTHING, wanted to experience the full range of Its creative potential. It did not want to know Itself only by serving others. It wanted to know Itself in all the ways that were possible. All forms and behaviors still come back to the Creator wanting to explore and know Its full range of potential, nothing more and certainly nothing less.

It is so easy to label things. This is good; this is bad. The Creator just IS. It is neither good nor bad. It is not compassionate, merciful, angry, or punishing. It simply IS. Those attributes (compassion, anger, etc.) are projections upon a field of pure consciousness that is simply experimenting with all the possible ways of expression that are available to It. It is BOTH serving Itself and serving others. It serves others by creating them and allowing them to participate in the experience It is having. It serves Itself by creating others through which It experiences. There is ONLY ONE LIFE being lived.

It is the Creator, in Its infinite array of forms or expressions.

That is the "absolute" way of looking at it. But you (and we) are also experiencing at the "relative" level of experience. Within that "relative" experience, there APPEARS to be "good" and "bad," STO and STS kinds of things and behaviors. They are "good" or "bad" only when compared to something else. That is the "relative" part—as one thing RELATES to (or refers to) something else. There is no way around this, as the Creator likes to play hide-and-seek with Itself, and so it hides in all forms while It seeks Itself. It makes things so much more interesting, as seen from the Creator's perspective, because there is so much more "grist for the mill." There is so much more to work with, and there is so much more variety available than there would be if things only came in one of these two flavors.

If there were only STO, things could get a little dull after awhile. If there were only STS, things wouldn't last very long, because the STS flavor, in serving only itself, is inherently predatory and destructive to everything else. It operates through competition, not cooperation. You can see the results on your own planet, which has been effectively destroyed by these self-serving behaviors on the part of so many.

But now we are at the time of Harvest, when each comes for their own and seeks to maximize their potential in the "great summing up" that is underway at this time. All of the Oversouls want to maximize their Light quotient, so their projections are going about gathering in more light of the flavor that they are made of. Both kinds of flavors are actively recruiting right now. The STS are seeking to increase their power, so they do what they can to increase the amount of fear in the environments in which they are operating. Fear gives them access, gives them power over those who are in fear. Since we have defined love (in part) as the absence of fear, you can see how love is the antithesis of what they would want you to feel in order to promote their agenda of gaining power. They can only gain power through others' fears, so wherever love is (as we have defined it), they are blocked from gaining power.

There are a great number of ETs interacting with Earth right now. They are here for many reasons—some to be active participants in the Harvest, and some to simply observe and learn from it. They come in both flavors. We are here to help you increase your Love and Light quotient. Others are here to increase fear and thus create more opportunities to increase their power over others. STS is always based on a master/slave hierarchical relationship. STS entities, regardless of origin, are always seeking to gain a foothold on someone else's shoulders so that they may gain power over others and climb up the rungs of their power hierarchy. STO is seeking to help other sovereign beings, to interact in ways that "level the playing field" and elevate *all* individuals to their maximum potential. STO revels in sharing the limitless wealth of the Creator's Love and Light, while STS seeks to accumulate as much of a "finite" amount of power as it can. The biggest laugh is that when viewed from the highest possible perspective, both flavors are seeking to become more like the Creator, but they seek it from opposite sides.

The Creator is the Source of all Love, Light, and Power. But the STO is not interested in power as much as it wishes to be *empowered* and to help others claim their "birthright," also—to share the limitless supply with others, because there is plenty for everyone. STS seeks to get, keep, and hoard as much power as it can, but the more successful it is, the lonelier it becomes. There actually comes a point when the STS is so lonely that it decides that it is tired of all that power, that the mere having of power is not satisfying when there is no one there to share it with. When an STS has reached that clarity of its position, then (and only then) its natural "next step" is to switch to the STO version of reality, and this is not as difficult as you might think. By the time an STS gets to that point, they have so thoroughly explored all the possible ways in which one gets and keeps power for itself, it has exhausted that set of possibilities. It has "been there, seen it, done it" with all of the possible experiences of that flavor and reached the end of its creative potential within that flavor, so it looks to the "greener pastures" of what it hasn't explored, jumps the fence, and quickly becomes an STO groupie.

ETs of both flavors are here to recruit (in the case of STS) or help (in the case of STO). The STS will try to keep those of the

STO persuasion from remaining on their path of growing love, because then the STS supply of power sources diminishes. Since STS is based on the idea of a FINITE supply, rather than the limitless abundance idea of the STO, any decrease in fear levels is perceived as a loss of power by the STS. That is why one sees so many well-intentioned individuals being "led astray" by STS entities. That is why love (as we have defined it) is the best armor and protection one can have and the greatest insurance policy one can get to make it on the STO path.

The media on your planet are not there to tell the truth. They are there to sell things, for that is how they get their portion of the power medium you call money. Fear sells. Sex sells. Romance sells. Emotion sells. Truth does not sell, except when it "exposes" something, and what is that but emotional titillation? The media is there to stimulate you to "buy" whatever it is that they are selling, whether it is a product, a philosophy (Who does it serve?), or a point of view that empowers you or (more likely) disempowers you.

The media has treated the subjects of ETs, UFOs, and "paranormal" phenomena in ways that increase the emotional titillation, the rush of adrenaline, also known as fear. Lately that has shifted a little, as there is more acceptance of higher realities, but on the whole the media serves the purposes of the STS flavor more than it does those of the STO flavor. It is natural that this would be the case, because the entire planetary economy is operating in ways that serve the STS individuals in high positions of authority more than it serves the general populace (which is so ignorant and unconscious of the consequences of their choices that they are easy pawns for the power-mongers above them).

We are here in great numbers, and when the time is right, we shall render ourselves visible to those who have "eyes to see," those whose frequency is that of love (as we have defined it), and can therefore see others who operate in that frequency. Those who are in fear will never see us. If you are in fear and see an ET, be assured it will be of the STS flavor. You cannot see love unless you are in that state of love, through the principle of resonance. But you can always FEEL love, even if you still contain some fear. So while you cannot see us yet, except with your inner vision, you can always FEEL us and our presence. You can also FEEL the feelings you get when STS energies are around you, whether they are of "human" or "ET" origin, whether they are in your visual frequency band or currently in frequencies beyond those your physical eyes can see.

Trust your feelings. We will say that again. *TRUST YOUR FEELINGS!* No matter what something "looks like" on the surface, ask yourself, "How does this FEEL to me?" There are many whose tongues drip with honey, who tell you what you want to hear, who put you to sleep with their hypnotic droning voices. But you can FEEL when you are being lulled, you can feel when you are being led astray. It is a subtle difference between that and moving out of fear on your own. You can be comforted when you are in pain, but only you can deal with your fears. You must face them down within yourself. No one can do that for you, although others can—by their example, advice, and encouragement—show you the way.

You are about to become ETs yourself, so it behooves you to become masters of your own feelings, to use your feeling capacity to detect who is playing what game. Do not rely on your media to tell you what is going on. Only your feeling sense and a willingness to examine the deeper levels of the surface phenomena will help you chart your course. In the end, though, you can never know enough to be safe. You must create your own sense of safety within yourself. Put your energy into creating that internal sanctuary, where you can connect with Source. But as you thread your way through these last days before the Harvest, know that there are those who would use you for their agenda, and there are those who are here to help you move through your fears into love (as we have defined it). It is up to you to choose in each and every moment, to move through your fears into love, as that is the ticket Home.

Those who are destined to go to Terra will need to have love in their hearts. It is not your deeds that matter as much as your frequency. If you have love and not fear, you will naturally behave in loving ways. If you ask for our help, we will give it in whatever ways and in whatever measure does not infringe on your own right to choose. There is an enormous amount of Grace available to help you move through your fear, but you must open yourself to receive it. Meditate. Breathe. Set aside some quiet time. Let the love come in. Let the fear go. You are safe. You cannot be destroyed. You do not have to "die." You are immortal beings, about to go on the adventure you have dreamed of, waking and sleeping. Terra calls.

We leave you now, in peace and honor and blessing. We shall speak to you again. Amen, Adonoy, Sabayoth. We are the Hosts of Heaven.

11

SUMMING UP
July 10, 1999

Today we wish to speak to you about the forthcoming Earth changes and the effects they will have upon the various lifeforms upon the planet. For some time now, we have been acting as conservators of certain species, to preserve them and their genetics for inhabiting the new planet, Terra. On Terra, everything will exist in an exalted state, not only in consciousness, but also in the forms that outpicture that changed consciousness. Every lifeform will be exquisite. Everything will be glorified, as Earth takes her rightful place as the jewel of the galaxy.

Toward this end, many of the species will be leaving the planet altogether. Those we have not collected, as they will no longer be present on Earth when she assumes her new form. These are principally those creatures that are part of the cycle of death, disease, and decay. There are some that will undergo a fundamental change in their nature, primarily those that have functioned as pets for humans, but others also. This is where the prediction that the "lion shall lie down with the lamb" comes from. Certain carnivores will change their essential nature in order to live on Terra and be part of that habitat.

Those aside, the other forms of life that are predators, disease-bearers, and those that participate in the breakdown of forms to more elemental forms will be absent. Everything else will be transformed or eliminated from the Terran "list" of lifeforms. (It should be noted that entirely new lifeforms, from other parts of the galaxy, will be "transplanted" to Terra, just as you transplant exotic plants into your gardens that are not native to your area.)

The Earth changes are part of this process. They serve several purposes. The first and primary purpose is as we stated: to cleanse the Earth of her accumulated burden of negativity—those thought-forms and energies that are of the lower frequencies and would keep her from her own ascension to the next frequency band of reality. The second purpose is to assist in the facilitation of getting all things to their own "right place." This is a special function being overseen by Archangel Michael and us, the Hosts of Heaven. (We are the "heavenly hosts" being spoken of in the expressions "Lord of Hosts" and the "Legions of Michael.") We have this special function to perform—to see to it that all things get to their "right place." You might think of us as traffic directors or logistics specialists. Your taxi and police dispatchers perform a similar function. They get the workers to the right spot at the right time to assist those who need assistance. The Earth changes serve other purposes, also, including making the third-density form of Earth uninhabitable for an extended period, so that the new world has all the attention it needs to be fully born.

We have spoken of Earth (and Terra) in terms of being the garden spot of the galaxy. In good stewardship of the land, each portion must be allowed to lie fallow for a time, in order for balance to be restored and nutrients to be replenished. The Earth has been sucked dry, all of her precious gifts mined beyond the state where they can naturally recover in a short period of time. You might say that humans have been living off their grandchildren's inheritance for some time, so the Earth changes will also serve to give Earth the very long period she needs to regain balance and restore herself. Those who are to inhabit the new Earth, Terra, will be housed in places that help them prepare for the new reality that they are to inherit. Terra is already in existence but not yet visible, as the human frequencies have not yet risen to the level they must be at to be able to perceive and experience her as a physical reality.

A time is coming in which all that has been built upon the

planet in terms of artificial structures will be leveled. Underground structures will not be so affected, but there is no point in looking to them for sustenance, as there will not be anything left alive on the surface. You can lay up stores of food, sources of energy, and implements, but you cannot prepare to live out the long period in which third density Earth will lie fallow. It is too long a time. The fourth density Earth—Terra—already exists, pristine, fertile, and exquisitely beautiful. Only those forms that are vibrating at that frequency will be compatible with her, so one cannot do anything but prepare to be one of those. Otherwise, you will experience a different outcome.

Not only the artificial structures will be leveled. In your scriptures, it says that the valleys will be raised up and the mountains laid low. This is the smoothing out of the planetary surface that we referred to, the elimination of the stored energies contained in the lines of stress in the crust called "faults." But Terra will be smooth for another reason. "Form follows function," is another of your sayings. As we have spoken before, Terra will be a fourth-density planet, of the STO orientation. In STO, everyone and everything is sovereign. It does not exist except to express itself within the context of the whole. There is no hoarding or accumulation of wealth by the few, for there is enough to be shared by all. And none shall experience poverty or want of any kind. In the elevated state of consciousness of Terra, all will live as royalty, for all will create whatever pleases them to create. The planet will be smooth to outpicture the smoothness of life, the equality of all within the Creation, and the total abundance that is available to those who are in alignment with Universal Laws.

We wish you to hear these things in the proper perspective. Nothing perishes. It only changes form. The form that is appropriate to Terra is the exalted version of what you see about you now. Things must either change or go somewhere else. The planet herself is about to change her form in drastic ways. These cataclysmic changes are the healing process that the planet must go through to achieve her destiny. It is all in Divine Order that this happens, and it is within Divine Order that it happens now, at this particular point in the planet's history. The window will open to provide the way, all the way back to Source. Everything that has been operating in the experience of separation consciousness must now either reconnect with Source or go somewhere else. To be on Terra, one will be in a perpetual state of Union with Source and thereby with all of Creation. Your senses will operate in the full spectrum of consciousness, not just the limited band you have available now.

It is principally because of the approaching Earth changes that we have come to give this series of Messages, so that you may view what is happening within the proper perspective. Many of you have been preparing for your roles for entire lifetimes, both in and before this one. That is why so many of you who are reading this Message have felt that you were here for some special purpose, why your mundane work in the world has sometimes left you wondering, "Is this all there is? Is this all I am going to do?" No, it is not all you are going to do, but your first task is your own transformation. Then and only then will you be equipped to go out and do the Creator's work for one another. Then and only then will you really be able to "help" with the great task at hand. Until then, your task is to open to receive. You are not in charge. You cannot do this for yourself. You can only open to receive what is being given.

We have urged you repeatedly to give your spiritual practice your highest priority. That is how you will open yourself to receive what is being offered to you at this time. Your Oversoul has "scheduled" you for many things in this transition. Relax and enjoy the ride! Your only other option is to resist it, and that will only result in discomfort for you. Why not "go with the flow"? Be like the river and simply stream through it all—liquid, unresisting and flowing. We can tell you that you will have much more fun that way. There is no way we can prepare you for all that lies ahead. We have tried our best to direct you to those activities and practices that will make your transition all that you would like it to be. The rest is up to you. If you resist, the pressures will build up until you surrender. Those who will not bend will break. There is help available at all times, but you must ask for it, as we cannot infringe upon your free will and choice. There is so much Grace flowing, if you will only be "gracious enough" to receive it.

Receive the gift. Do not turn away and think you are not worthy of it. You are the children of the dawn, the architects, builders, and occupants of Terra, the new Earth. Receive the gift and be humble and grateful for this opportunity to serve, to experience, and to be there when the curtain goes up on the new stage for the new drama. Terra will truly be the embodiment of "Heaven on Earth." We are so grateful to you for being willing to take on the garment of flesh, to anchor those incoming energies that are streaming in now in ever-increasing amounts, and to act as living lightning rods to ground them into the planet so that she may rise and ascend to her destined station—Terra, the jewel of the galaxy. We look forward to working with you further. Until then, we shall sign off for now, but know that we are with you always. We are the "rod and the staff" that will comfort you and sustain you, through all that lies ahead. Each and every one of you precious beings is surrounded by angels, whose only function is to protect you, love you, and guide you—to lead you Home.

Amen, Adonoy Sabayoth. We are the Hosts of Heaven.

12

SIGNS ALONG THE WAY
June 21, 2000

Well, now. It is almost a year since we last spoke with you. Being that today is the summer solstice—that time when the flow of life on Earth completes its upward movement from the depths of the winter solstice into the sun of the day, and turns upon itself once more to begin the journey downward, toward the heart of darkness, toward the next solstice which will mark the beginning of winter—it seemed like an appropriate time to begin our next series of conversations with you. Is it not strange, this ever-swinging movement between the dark to the light and back to the dark again? Yet it is in the nature of things on planet Earth for it to do this. Now—just as the summer comes on—so do thoughts and energy begin to contemplate and anticipate the approach of winter again.

Darkness is but a part of the cycle of life, and these "dark days" that mark the ending of the planetary cycle in 3D shall give rise to a time of incredible light, an eternal springtime for the planet and all that are upon her. We remind you of this. Do not forget it. For just as the darkness now comes, the light is already born within it. These Messages are meant to be a positive pole for you to carry within your hearts, to balance the negative that will be expressing all around you. Walk in the light. Carry the light. Be the embodiment of light and you will find the path before you is an easy one, even if all about you is coming down to its extermination.

We have called this Message, "Signs Along the Way," and it is our intention to give you some understanding of the path that lies directly before you. The Earth changes have begun now in earnest, although they are still mild compared to what will follow. You will notice that the clusters of earthquakes have been fairly constant now, and that they are of a consequential magnitude that should cause the world to take notice, but they are still asleep. It is ho-hum and not news, so long as it does not cause destruction of property and life. Note that property is valued even above life, and the loss of property is always mentioned in reporting the consequences of Nature's ways. And so now, while these beginning tremors are occurring at record rates, there is no mention of them in the news. They are not considered to mean anything. But they DO mean something. They mean that the time of which we spoke is now at hand.

In addition to the earthquakes, there is also the weather, the fires and floods, and other weather-related phenomena. These, too, are signs of the times of which we spoke. The weather patterns have been changing for a long time, but now they are noticeably NOT "normal." Even so, while some areas suffer, others experience uncharacteristically benevolent weather. It is that same pattern of a "mixed blessing" that shall characterize so much of the times ahead. While some things are destroyed and some people fall upon hard times, at the very same time, new and beautiful things will come into being and people who had been struggling will begin to prosper. Many things will change, and not in ways that you might expect!

YOU are changing, too, and if you are paying attention, you will notice that your perceptions are changing, too. Your senses are heightened and attuned to more beauty in life. The landscape and living things seem to be brighter somehow. Foods taste better or worse to you, depending on how well you have chosen them. Those of a lower vibration or which are prepared by people who resent having to cook them will taste worse, or make you feel bad after you eat them. Those which are lovingly grown and prepared, and for which you express your appreciation, will not only taste better but they will make you feel more nourished than those which have been "thrown together" or grabbed along the way in a busy day. To the extent that you honor your own being enough to select the best foods and eat them with appreciation, to that extent you will be increasing your "Light quotient" and shine more brightly. In loving and giving to yourself, you are in a sense honoring and praising the Source which creates you. Think about it. If someone gave you a beautiful cake, into which they had put the costliest and most delicious ingredients, would you throw it on the ground, grind it under your heel, and so despise the gift?

Hopefully, you would not. If you were perceptive, you would see how much care went into the creating of that cake and you would bow in reverence before the baker for the preciousness of the gift. Your own bodies are the "bread" that has been formed by the Creator. Your own bodies are made of the most precious ingredients, and no matter how you have been treated by your earthly travels and those who were part of your journey, you are still a precious gift to the universe. Honor that gift and treat yourself with love and respect. Eat well of the best quality foods—those which were raised with love and consciousness, which were prepared with love and attention, and which fit with your own dietary needs. This will not only give you the best nutrition to support your bodies in their transformation, you will also be giving your bodies the message that you care about them and they will support you in return. You can experience a great deal of rejuvenation and healing through simply choosing well and making it a priority to do so.

Nonetheless, there are some discomforts to be endured. The body you presently occupy will be the one that takes you across the light bridge between this world and the next. All your other parallel lives are being terminated, and the cellular memories that you carry in all of your tissues are being purged. Your relationship to time is changing. Your minds often become a blank at the most annoying times. You feel like your head is made of cotton wool a lot of the time, and you may wonder how you will get anything done. You need a lot of sleep and are drinking a lot more water (hopefully, very pure water!). You may be gaining weight, losing weight, growing hair, losing hair—the process is very individual, but the one thing that will be "common" to all is that you are changing.

Your sleep patterns will vary a great deal. You may sleep very deeply or you may be restless without knowing why. Your bodies may feel like they are vibrating at times, especially if you wake up during the night, between periods of sleep. You may have changes in bowel habits, or changes in the foods that you want to eat. Be gentle with yourselves, and take care of yourselves. For those of you who are usually so busy taking care of others and their needs, this is going to require that you put yourself "first," which is a change in itself! If you have emotions rising to the surface, do whatever you can to facilitate their release without wallowing in them or getting caught up in dramas. Use whatever works for you—singing, toning, writing, warm baths—whatever you find is the most natural and supportive way for you to move through the purging of your cellular memory and the associated emotions of your various experiences.

For those of you who have had a difficult life (and that is most of you), let yourself now feel the pain of those times when you had to simply keep going and feelings were shunted aside so that you could cope. Let that pain surface gently and watch it pass through you and out of you, like you were looking into a fishbowl and seeing streams of cloudy water swirling through and then disappearing. You have all experienced a lot of pain, and whatever you must now feel and let pass through you on its way out of you, let it all go. You will lose a sense of identity as this healing proceeds. You will not be sure of who you are anymore, because it is from this personal "history" of pain that you have decided who and what you are and who and what you aren't. The truth is—at its most fundamental level—everything you see and feel, everything you saw and felt, IS YOU. But in moving into this larger, less defined interpretation of Self, you will lose the benchmarks from which you defined yourself in the past.

You will feel less connected with some people, more connected with others, as you move toward the poles of your destiny and merge your being and energies with those of your true family—your brothers and sisters in the many mansion worlds of the One Infinite Creator. WE are that family, and you are preparing to shed your old skins and put on your garments of Light. When you have done that, you shall stand among us as equals and we shall be able to embrace each other once again. We look forward to that day as much as you do, for we know how much joy we shall all have in that reunion.

We leave you now in peace and honor and blessing and we shall talk with you again. It is time to come home.

We love you so much. We would hope that you can come to love yourselves, as well. Amen, Adonoy Sabayoth. We are the Hosts of Heaven.

13

IT'S ALL GOD
June 22, 2000

"In the beginning, God created the heavens and the Earth." This is what it says; this is how it is written in the scriptures with which you are so familiar. But it is not really how it was.

In the beginning there was God, and God was and IS "All There Is." It is still God. And so God did not, in that sense, create anything that is not God. There is a tendency to view the Creation as both a product of and separate from the Creator. But this is an impossibility. The very being and substance of the Creator penetrates all form and is indeed an expression, an outgrowth as it were, of the one body. Just as you have hairs on your head or lashes on your eyelids, so it is with every form of Creation: they are springing forth from the single body, from God.

We who speak to you are but a facet of that one Creator; you are but a facet of that one Creator. It is God who speaks through you and through us, because we are all God. That is not to say that we ARE the Creator, but rather a part of the Creator, an expression of the Creator, a form that resides WITHIN the Creator. Nothing is outside of God, you know, but this is an expression that is limited by the language of words. When you are on Terra, you will have the full experience of being totally in oneness with the Creator, where your body will be experiencing itself as constantly emerging from the substance of the Creator, the matrix and ground of all being and form.

95

And so this Creator interpenetrates all things. All things have consciousness. All things are part of that Creator. Now look about you, to your beautiful planet and see the devastation upon one part of the Creator by another part of the Creator. Is this not madness? Would you mutilate your own body if you were aware of what you were doing? We think not. And yet that is what has happened to this beautiful planet and continues to happen, even now, at this late hour.

The forests are being felled at a record rate. It is almost like a feeding frenzy, as the last giants of the forest are toppled to build yet more products for yet more people, and so it goes. Even the smaller trees are being harvested in this mad rush to consume, consume, consume, until there is nothing left.

Yes, we have spoken of the Earth changes. Yes, they are underway as we speak now. But even if there were no Earth changes, this mad rush to claim for oneself the last of the dwindling resources of Earth would soon render the planet unfit for all life, most particularly for human habitation. So, in some ways, the Earth changes are a merciful thing, to stop the process from proceeding to the place where untold suffering would be the result.

There has been enough killing; there has been enough eradication of species. And if humankind is to progress, and survive, and THRIVE, this desecration of this beautiful planet must end, and soon, before it is all way too late.

But it is all in Divine order. These are all parts of the experiment that was ordained from the foundation of the Creation. These apparent destructions are still the Will of God, which is sometimes difficult to understand for those who are still in separation. But when you are no longer in separation, you will be in a place where one can see, understand, feel, and embrace the wholeness of it, without getting caught up in the drama of it.

And so Earth is in her final hour of her travail, and humankind is dancing at the last big party. Many there are who are aware or sensing at some level of their being that the end is near, and so there is an apparent disregard for what is prudent and a kind of reckless abandon to consume yet even more. There is complaint about the high price of gas, and quarreling about how difficult it is to have to pay such high prices. What will the tumult be if the gas is no longer available? And that is surely an outcome. The supplies are not infinite. Yes, they are vast, but so is the sea of humanity, and the demand for more and more oil is insatiable.

It is also very destructive—of the environment, of the air, of the waters. The oil is used to create so many things that do not degrade once they are discarded, so you are burying yourself in your own filth, in your own refuse. The tragedy is that what was once a beautiful garden is gradually being turned into a garbage dump. What a desecration! And yet, it was all foreseen. It is now time for that to come to a close, and it will not be a gentle birth, because of the tensions that remain in the Earth's crust, reflecting her absorption of so much negative energy.

We have not yet touched on the heart of the matter. We are, in a sense, preparing the stage for the drama that will now unfold. It is almost time for the cataclysms, and we want to prepare you and prepare you well for what to expect, and how things will go for those who are destined for Terra and those who are not. If you are among those who are destined for Terra, you will be witnessing a rather strange sight, for as the world around you crumbles and dissolves into entropy and death, you will find yourselves prospering and moving up to a new level of abundance, joy, and well-being. It is you who have suffered for so long, and now it is your time in the light. And those who have become inebriated on the excess of consumption will now pay that price.

We do not say that in judgment, but rather as assessing the situation for what it is. The preliminary earthquakes have come and gone, and now there will be a brief pause and then the next level of cleansing will take place. Soon, your news media will not be able to ignore the phenomena of Earth changes. It will be in everyone's face. There will be an increase in concern and fear as these things unfold and become more established as a pattern, rather than isolated events. You might think that the Earth—through these various small earthquakes—could release sufficient crustal tension, that it will not have to result in anything more severe. However, there is such an accumulation of negative thought energy that has been absorbed by the planet that it all must be purged.

Even as your own bodies are being purged, so must the Earth's body be purged and cleansed.

And so this will result in Earth changes and geophysical events, not only of a much greater magnitude than is normally experienced, but also a greater frequency and persistence. This first cluster is essentially over, with a few isolated aftershocks. However, in a time that is very soon at hand, no later than July, we shall be witnessing the next level of cleansing at the Earth level, which will take several forms. Not only will there be tectonic movement and volcanic eruptions, but there will be other types of things, as foretold in the Book of Revelation in the Bible.

There will be many strange phenomena in Nature. There will be a rain of "plagues" akin to that described in the time of Egypt, in the story of Moses, and there is much sorrow coming in the cleansing of the planet because she has absorbed so much sorrow that she does not want to carry any more, nor does it serve for her to carry it. For what she is becoming is Terra, the glorious jewel in the crown of Creation, and in which there is no place for sorrow and tears, only joy and love, and all these matters of the third density shall soon pass away.

The cleansing will be complete this time, not partial as in other times, for none of the old can be taken into the new. You yourselves are being purged of your cellular memory and so it is with the Earth. The Earth is a living being, and her body is riddled with "dis-ease" over all the things that have been done to her, plus having absorbed all the pain and sorrow of the thoughtforms that have been experienced or projected by humankind. And the pain and sorrow of the animals is felt also. Many of you do not realize that animals are fully conscious and do have bonds among them and do have energetic exchange in their own form of communication. So animals are not rightfully your slaves, or pets, or possessions, and on Terra, all animals will be free.

And so now we would speak to you of the times ahead. In the very shorter term, there will be increased disturbances and ruptures, not only in geophysical changes, but also in the fabric of society. The tension is growing, the clamor for people to "do something" is rising, and there is great discontent growing in the face of apparent prosperity. There are dark clouds gathering, economically and socially. There are going to be eruptions, like boils of a disease. There will be cleansings within the populations of Earth, as well as the planet. There are going to be strange diseases, of a mental, emotional, and physical nature—many plagues of many kinds. Some will be engineered by humankind and those of a despotic nature, and some will be mutations of existing microbes, as a result of the changing frequency and the increasing amount of higher-frequency light, known to you as the ultraviolet. The hole in the ozone layer is of course part of the equation, and is man-created, but once again, we would say that ALL of this has been scheduled and is by a combined, collective soul choice.

All of you who have been battling for the light, and carrying the light, and pleading to be heard, and all of those of you who have tried to stop the destruction and the devastation and the greed and the corruption—all of you have labored and labored well, but it seems that evil (or what you would call as "evil") will have its day. Once again, we would remind you that this is all *of* the Creator and is the Creator-in-expression. It is difficult from your perspective of separation to understand how a loving or benevolent Creator could allow such things to happen, or that such a beautiful planet would be sacrificed in such a way. But this story HAS a happy ending, and we wish to remind you of that.

The Creator, being the Creator, wishes to experience everything, not just the things that are pleasurable. It wants to explore ALL the possibilities, all the combinations and permutations, and indeed this causes much apparent suffering. But there is also a place for joy in this Creation. It is in short supply upon your planet at the moment, but that will radically change after the shift.

And so now we return to the days ahead. There will be much, much disharmony, disruption, chaos, fear, destruction, loss of life, loss of property, loss on all sides—or so it will seem. But at the same time, those of you who are destined for Terra will find yourselves prospering and enjoying a much happier state of affairs than you have in the years leading up to now. We wish to support you in your last days on Earth and make them pleasurable, for you have served and served well, and now it is time to "gather the troops," as it were, and to call them home. For the homecoming will be taking place in a matter of 3 to 4 years of your time. There is a coming home to oneself that is a part of this, and a coming home to your rightful estate as co-creators of this marvelous universe, and also a coming home to the places that nourish your heart and wipe away your tears.

We wish to have you among us again, our brothers and sisters, and we are your soul family. We are YOUR brothers and sisters, as well. You are totally our equal and have been valiant in your service and your willingness to take on the garment of flesh, but soon it will be time for you to move up and move on, and to put on your garment of Light and become the gods and goddesses that you are. It will be a wonderful time for you, and the blessings will never cease.

Now, the dark days ahead lead to a new dawning, and the first rays of that dawning are already visible. Much work has gone in. Much has been accomplished. Many have turned to the light, and if not with full understanding or full discernment, still much has been accomplished. Those of you who are originating from the higher realms will be regaining your estate, and soon—by our standards, anyway. Consider that it has been a 4 1/2-billion-year walk and 3 or 4 years is but a blink of the eye in that kind of time scale. We would ask you to realize that we are ever with you. Nothing happens by accident. There are no accidents. Everything is an outpicturing of God, and everything contains within it the seeds of its own completion. We shall speak more on these matters, but that is all for now.

Amen Adonoy Sabayoth, We are the Hosts of Heaven.

14

THE CROSSING-POINT
July 27, 2000

Yesterday—July 26, 2000—marked an important milestone on the journey to Terra. We prefer to call it "the crossing-point," because it marked the shift from the funneling-inward movement (that has been going on since the Earth was formed) to a funneling-outward movement that represents the expansion into the new reality. You are perhaps familiar with the spiral shape that describes evolution: each turn on the spiral sees a return to past themes and issues, but at a new level, enriched by the lessons of prior experience. But there can be a spiraling inward as well, in which the "lessons" of the past—in the form of memories and imprinting—are thrown off as the spiral tightens toward a "zero point" at which it has no circumference at all.

Yesterday marked that point at which the inward spiral reached its maximum compression and began to turn in the opposite direction. Now instead of throwing off old memories and imprinting, it will gather into itself altogether new experiences and expressions, none of which have been ever experienced on 3D Earth in all of her history. This is the time of the ingathering, of the harvesting of all that has gone before and the receiving of the "gifts of the kingdom." For you who are destined for Terra, this will come as a great relief, for so many of you have endured much suffering and hardship of all kinds. Now, however, that has served and will pass away. Now is your time to embody the riches that belong to those who serve the One Infinite Creator so wholeheartedly, and it will be a welcome time for you all, to be sure.

It will not come in all at once. Just as the spiral wound inward over long stretches of time, so will its expansion wind outward over long stretches of time. However, from the shape of the spiral, you can see that near its point, the turns are shorter and therefore come closer together in time. Just as you have experienced an inner acceleration as the spiral turned ever faster in its cycles toward the "zero point," now that the "crossing-point" has been achieved, the initial cycles will be very fast at first and gradually slow down as the turns encompass more and more "territory." In the beginning, you will not notice how much has changed. An entire new paradigm was anchored in but because the sweep of the spiral is so limited so close to the crossing-point, it will be some time before you notice how different your lives are becoming. At first it will be a very subtle thing, more felt than seen, but in a relatively short time, it will be unmistakable.

The spiral has spanned more than 4 billion of your years, and the outward journey will take at least as long to complete the innate symmetry [which mirrors the inward spiral]. However, since the outward movement is an expansion, it really can go on forever, as there will never be another "crossing-point" for this Creation. It is really about going beyond ALL limitation, and therefore the expansion phase is without limits—essentially infinite in nature. Rather than CONTRACT BACK into the Godhead, you will EXPAND AND EXPAND until you MERGE with that Godhead in its infinite scope and expression. You will embody more and more Light until you are just Light. Every vestige of dense materiality will dissolve into pure Light and consciousness, but that is a journey of billions of your years—hard for you to relate to or imagine.

So now it is here—the time for which you have prepared for so many lifetimes, in so many guises. This is the last of your dense physical expressions and from here you will only become more and more filled with Light. We would remind you that this is a process, not an "event," so the change will be gradual but certain. There will come a time when you will have to be lifted off of the planet's surface and held aside while all else plays out to completion. We will be assisting in this, but it is a partnership between us, not a "rescue mission." You carry your responsibility in the equation, too, and it has required much of you in the past. Now it only requires that you open to receive what is yours to receive. That may bring up some issues for some of you—issues of self-worth and conflicts about what it "looks like" to be a "server." There has been much conditioning in your religions that you are small and unworthy and must place your hopes in an outside force or being to "save you" from your earthly imperfections. But in our eyes you are ALREADY PERFECT, and all that is needed is for you to open and gratefully receive your "birthright" as the sons and daughters of the Creator.

Those who are not bound for Terra will have a different experience, and many of them will go through trials and suffering as they move to their poles of destiny. Remember that everyone is operating according to their soul's choice. Do not feel superior to them, as you are only manifesting your soul's choice also, and all souls are equal in the Creation. They are all just aspects of the One Creator, so how can they be other than perfect? How could any aspect of the Creator be more or less important than any other aspect? It is ALL God-in-expression, as we told you last time. Just surrender to your destiny path and give thanks for the goodness that now comes to you. And allow everyone else to do the same [with regard to THEIR destiny path].

If you feel moved to help out during others' travail, by all means help out. But don't do it out of guilt or to "earn points in Heaven." It is perfectly all right for you to simply enfold them in your love and light and not do anything outwardly to hinder their process or movement toward their destiny. In time, when you do indeed turn your faces toward Terra and leave your beloved 3D Earth behind, none of this will matter any more. You will have surrendered up all attachments to your past identities and will gladly embrace the "new world" that is yours to experience. But that is enough about that for now. It is still some time away, and there is much to enjoy and explore and create in the meantime. Rejoice now, where you are and how you are, for this IS your last lifetime in dense physicality and you now have an opportunity to enjoy it before leaving it behind forever.

We leave you now in peace, and honor, and blessing. Amen, Adonoy Sabayoth. We are the Hosts of Heaven.

15

THE COMING STORM
September 21, 2000

Now is the time of which we have spoken. This is the time in your year when the day and night are of equal lengths, but soon the night will be longer and the day shorter. So it is that the darkness will appear to increase and the light to diminish, but just as the sun is always shining behind the clouds, so is the dawn waiting beyond the night. And so it is now.

You are entered upon a time when there will be much confusion, fear, and "darkness," for what is darkness but a lack of understanding? All that you would call "darkness" or "evil" is but a lack of understanding, and so it is never a permanent condition, but while it is in operation, it can cause much suffering for many. And so it is now. There are those upon your planet who would call themselves "human," but in their actions, thoughts, and words would appear to be some kind of monster—without feelings for others or others' pain and suffering. The "love quotient" in these individuals is nearly absent, but that is part of their learning, too. Think of the one you called Hitler. Was he enlightened? Was he happy? Was he satisfied with what his life brought him?

The answer is clearly "No." And so the soul of this one you called Hitler is still on the inner planes, mulling over the effects of that life, trying to understand what went so horribly wrong. You each have incarnated to gain certain understandings, and it is no different for those of the STS persuasion than it is for those of the STO orientation. You are each trying to understand, which is made more difficult by the fact that you are veiled. So, as you see what to you might seem the height of foolish behavior, remember that these are souls who are simply trying to understand why things aren't working very well for them. Even those who consider themselves to know what is "best" for everyone are going to be challenged in the days ahead.

Everything is about to change and change radically. People have different ways of trying to cope with change. Some seek constructive and cooperative solutions; others seek to withdraw and arm themselves against all possibilities. Each of these kinds of choices leads to more understanding. In the end, one has to surrender totally to the fact that one simply can't know everything, and then one has to let go and let God show the way. THEN "miracles" can occur, but not as long as one thinks it is within their hands to "make it happen."

Those who have positioned themselves as the power elite on your planet have laid grand plans to take over everything and profit from it. However, as much power as they have amassed, it is only based on economics. As long as the economic system operates and people have to depend on it for their needs, the power elite will have an easy time of putting into place their plans for world domination. However, this would be a violation of everyone else's choices, and this particular time in Earth's course is all about choices, so the Earth herself will be a major factor in keeping things more equal so that everyone has the opportunity to choose.

There are major storms coming—economic, geophysical, and political. People will be challenged to make a choice: will they act for self-preservation or will they work together to help one another? You who read and cherish these Messages will be spared the worst part of things, as a rather dramatic occurrence will be coming for you in the very near future (that is a relative term, of course, as time has no meaning for us in the higher dimensions—it is always "now."). In the near future, as you are lifted in your vibration, you will experience yourself as living in a very different kind of reality. It will not be an abrupt shift, but a gradual dawning in your awareness that things are not the same somehow. At the same time, there will be a threshold that can be felt by those who are sensitive to such things, and you will be safely across the barrier that separates the third density from the fourth.

Make no mistake: this will only happen for those who are attuned to and aligned with these Messages. The others who have chosen Terra but are not yet awakened will endure the effects of the coming storms as part of their process of personal cleansing and the opportunity to refine their choice for the positive path. It is all designed to bring maximum benefit to all—those who would choose now and those who will choose later. It is all about increased understanding, and the power elite will have their "lessons," too.

This birth will be a difficult one for most of the people on your planet, of all persuasions. Even the STS will be challenged to deal with the changing circumstances and the destruction of their well-laid plans. You see, it is all a house of cards, built upon technology that is vulnerable to being disrupted through any number of occurrences. One well-aimed burst from the sun could wipe out all of the communication satellites and bring down virtually all international commerce. The sun is a player in this equation, too.

There are other ways that the system can be disrupted. Weather will play a big part in things, and crop failures are not the only consequence. However, this is going to "hurt" the "little people" more than the rich and powerful, so that will not be as big a factor as some other things in the shorter term. The power elite are not invulnerable, but it is some time before they will be brought down. In the interim, they will appear to have their day to rule, and they will be given the opportunity to gain greater understanding of the nature of the path they have chosen. Since it is ALL GOD, there are other apparently separate individuals who will be providing them with the opportunity to learn their "lessons" firsthand, while at the same time gaining their own understanding about the best ways to not become victims under the crushing machinations wielded by the power elite. STS is always trying to enslave others; STO wishes to be free and to throw off the yoke of oppression, wherever they find it.

And so a clash between these two opposing forces—those who would enslave and those who would be free—is inevitable. It will take many forms, not the least of which is your familiar "war." However, there will be "wars" fought in other ways and in other fields of endeavor. Truth will battle with falsity. Love will strive with fear. Each person will have many opportunities to choose—moment by moment, day by day—and in so choosing to make their collective choice for one path or the other.

There are many parallel futures to emerge from the platform of third-density Earth. Each one is a "layer" that vibrates with a certain frequency, similar to the bands of color in your visible spectrum. However, the spectrum is continuous, with one color flowing into another, and these parallel futures will ultimately separate from each other into distinct and unique worlds of experience. We have spoken of the very small percentage that will end up on Terra. There are many "slices" that will be cut off the single "loaf" that constitutes your present reality. The most beneficial thing you can do for yourselves is to focus entirely on yourself and your choices. Whatever you do, feel into those choices in each and every moment of the day, each and every day, and choose what seems "right" to you to do in that moment. You are dealing with a wave of change and the discipline is to "surf" that wave by remaining totally present—neither in the future or the past—so as not to lose your balance by leaning too far forward or backward.

It will be a time when you will find yourself remembering all that led you to the present moment, and you will have faith built upon remembering all that you have already gone through, but each time that you have followed that thread of the past to a natural completion point, gently bring yourself back into the present moment, just like a dog shakes itself off after a swim in a lake. Just so, if you find yourself drifting into daydreams of the future—when they have come to a natural end, bring yourself gently back into the present and focus on what is squarely before you to do in that moment. This is the way you will walk: one step at a time, moment by moment, learning to live in the NOW.

We will close by returning to the title of this Message: "The Coming Storm." The way you will survive and THRIVE during these times is to remain fixed in the present moment. Trust in the Creator to guide you perfectly through to your destination. While many will seem to suffer, you will be lifted free of all of that, in order to serve later on, when those who remain will need your assistance. We shall have more to say on that topic, but for now, we leave you in peace and honor and blessing. Amen, Adonoy Sabayoth. We are the Hosts of Heaven.

16

ALLOW ALL THINGS
September 28, 2000

In the beginning, there was no-thing. Then arose a thought and out of that thought all things came into being. At first, there was only harmony, but not much "progress" was made, because while all things were in harmony, there was not much impetus for change or exploration of alternative paths. The Thinker of the thought noticed this, and It thought another thought. This second thought introduced the idea of opposites, which could clash and therefore produce striving. All that you see around you now is a result of that striving.

If all had remained as One, nothing of the richness you see in your lives would have occurred. A great abundance of forms and a great abundance of possibilities thus was created, and the original thought was greatly expanded by this choice on the part of the Thinker, but also at a great price. Know you the expression, "the pearl of great price"? This is the price of which we speak.

As things unfold upon your planet and in your time, these two opposites will increase their movement toward opposite poles. All that is in the middle will either move to the poles or perish, in order to begin again on another world where they will have more opportunities to explore the choice of the opposites. When we say "perish," however, we refer only to their physical bodies. Their Oversouls will persist and simply put forth other projections of themselves into the worlds that await on the other side of the shift.

ALL Oversouls are withdrawing their projections now, so even for those who will ride this shift intact, in the vehicle that they presently occupy, there will only be one projection from the Oversoul that rides the wave of change. How, then, are you to view all this, and what will be the process and experience of going first to the poles and then to your destined exit path from 3D Earth to 4D Terra?

To begin with, there will be an intensification of the polarities. Those who are inclined toward the positive, or STO pole will become more so, and those who are inclined toward the negative, or STS pole will also become more so. This creates the maximum energetic potential, but it also creates the greatest disharmony, IF the two poles interact. How can you experience this journey with the least amount of friction? You disengage from fighting the negativity and withdraw into a world that is solely of your pole, that is totally harmonious for you.

"But what about evil?" you cry. What you call evil is but a choice. Do you remember the teaching in the Bible to "resist not evil"? In order to have the smoothest transition to your destined outcome, you must allow all things. You must allow all choices, and that includes the choice for the negative path. If you engage with "evil," you bind your energies to conflict and you cannot experience peace and harmony while you are fighting against someone else's choice. Allow all things. Allow all soul choices. Allow, allow, allow.

Many of you refer to those whom you call Masters. We would say to you that OUR definition of a Master is one who is so expanded in their understanding that he or she takes in ALL within them, within their embrace, and holds it without preference, without saying or feeling that any part is better than any other part. When you are fully born into your new awareness, a great understanding will fill you. You will "see" for the first time since taking on the veil which hides the truth from your sight. You will see all things in their right place and in their right meaning. But for now, you only see part of the picture, so in remembering that there is more going on than what you can perceive, you will again be called to surrender and to allow all things. You are not in charge. You are not the force that drives the creation forward. But you are an aspect of this force in action, and therefore you WILL at some point regain the full understanding of the nature of that force and your own true nature.

Until then, until you do have full understanding, recognize and accept that your understanding is to one degree or another limited, and so allow all things, for you do not know their hidden purpose. You do not know how it serves. If you are ASKED, then by all means respond as you feel is right to do. But more will be saying and telling than will be asking. More will be shouting and even screaming in their fear than will be asking. If someone asks, then and only then should you answer, but if no one is asking, remain in your center and rooted in the truth of your being and your choice for the pole you have chosen.

Resist not evil. Resist not anything. Surrender to the higher intelligence that guides your every step and simply ask when you have doubts of your own, "How shall I be with this (situation)? What is right action here?" But always come from your center, your knowing about what is true for you. Be content to make your own choice for yourself, and allow others to do the same. What does it gain if you try to "rescue" someone? You have only delayed their opportunity to make their own choices.

On Terra all will be sovereign. To be sovereign means to be willing to be totally alone in one's own understanding, to be beyond being able to be coerced or manipulated. Many great sages and warriors in many traditions have had this quality. You must be warriors now, only warriors in the sense of standing firm in the midst of the impending chaos, not in resisting any of that which will now play out. Be calm in the midst of the storm. Keep breathing. Meditate. Keep grounding the Light that is streaming in to the planet now. Keep opening the channel of your bodies and ground the Light into the planet. Empty out until you are like a hollow reed, able to simply allow all things to pass through you. The cleansing is underway and will accelerate with the passage of time. Allow, allow, allow.

You are yet asleep, but you are awakening. When you have fully awakened, the reality you will see will not be the reality that others who are still sleeping and striving with each other will see. You will float beyond all that. You will experience total calm, peace, and harmony, even while the storm rages all around you. You will be centered in peace and harmony, even while all things are coming apart around you. Soon, you will not even notice, because you will be fascinated with something else. A beautiful light will beckon to you and you will follow it. You will be going home.

Amen, Adonoy Sabayoth. We are the Hosts of Heaven.

A WORD OF EXPLANATION: I normally don't comment on individual Messages, but I have received the same question from several people, so I thought I'd add a note of explanation to the above. To "allow" all things is not to be confused with passivity or being a victim. The Message is talking about NOT JUDGING something as "evil," and becoming detached and expanded enough to see things from the "isness" point of view. Everything is just being what it IS. When one is in full consciousness, one can "see" all things for what they ARE. However, the Masters do not accept assaults on their person. There are at least two times that Y'shua/ Jesus literally disappeared from the midst of an angry crowd, and the Masters in *The Life and Teachings of the Masters of the Far East** stood upon the parapets of a town and repelled the invading brigands by reflecting their hostile energies back upon them. You are always responsible for your own actions, and your inner voice and intuition will tell you what is "right action" if you can listen to it. There is no need to accept harm to yourself or loved ones. "Allowing" here means to allow everyone to make their soul choices and to not judge one or the other path as being better than any other. They all lead back to God.

_____

* See "Suggested Reading" on page 139.

17

THE NEW MILLENNIUM
November 21, 2000

It is now late in the year 2000 and the millennium is drawing to a close. It has been a long journey and many expected that the big shift would occur on January 1 of the year 2000, but the big shift is just ahead. It does not matter what was done or when the dates of your calendar system were adjusted. The fact remains that in the consensus reality of the majority of your world's population, this numbering system is in use and accepted as the reality, and therefore has the energy of reality for all of those who accept it. Given that picture, the new millennium is about to ring in, and with it will come many changes. The different realities are already well along the course of separating from each other, and that will continue. However, for those that are destined for Terra, the shift into the new reality has already begun and will become much more apparent from January 1 of 2001 onward.

There has been a substantial acceleration in recent months, since the crossing-point of July 26 was reached and passed. Now the spiral will turn more slowly, but each turn will take in noticeably greater amounts of change. The DEGREE of change will increase, even as the RATE of change decreases. What that means is that if you look back from today to July 26, it will not seem that your life has changed all that much from how it was then, but you felt that things were accelerating tremendously. Once the change from the old millennium to the new is accomplished, it will feel quite different.

You will feel like you are "floating," and are gently supported in a sort of bubble, one in which you are insulated from the clamor of the world around you. At first, it will only seem like things have gotten much more quiet inside of you, something like what it is like when you totally immerse yourself in water and the sounds of the world become muffled and unimportant. However, as things proceed, it will become apparent to you that your EXPERIENCE of life is different in ways that you cannot now anticipate. You might even doubt that you are awake, because it will all take on a sort of dreamlike quality. It is important to tell you now that you should not attempt to re-engage with the life that is falling away from you. Just let yourself float gently upward and let yourself experience the total calm and support that surrounds you in this ocean of consciousness. Turn off the exterior stimuli and leave them for the "madding crowds." If you need to let go of people, circumstances, or certain "conditions" in your life, do so with ease and grace and do not engage in blame in order to justify the separating out into your own reality and destiny path. Just simply let go of how you are holding on to them, just like you were a balloon, tethered to them by a piece of string, only now you can choose to let go of your end of the piece of string and thereby float upward.

This is a process, not an "event," so you are already in the "orb of influence" (to use an astrological term). You will begin to feel the disconnect if you let it come to you easily and without resistance or fear. We are lifting you into the next level of vibration and it will feel a little strange to you, but trust the process and your own "knowing." Let the tumult fade away and receive the peace of the Light that floods over you and pours into your cells. You are dropping your material density and moving up to the next level. You will experience shifts in your perception of yourself. Do not resist them. Let go easily and let yourself become a more clear representation of your essence.

You each have an essence that is the expression of the "tones" of your Oversoul. As you let go of the identity you had and let your-self become this closer approximation of your individual aspect of the Creator, you will experience the pleasure of becoming just exactly that person that you most want to be. It will be an inner experience at first, but it will also show up on the surface, where it can be seen by others with "eyes to see." It will be FELT by those around you who cannot "see" it, and they might have some distress or feeling that they are "losing" you. They might experience fear and try to stop what it is they perceive of as the cause of the fear—your change—but all you need to do is love them, let them be how they are, give them what reassurance you can to comfort them that everything is all right, and let yourself drift upwards anyway. You will be in the company of those like yourself, and there will be comfort in that for you, but in the meantime, you must be kind as you take your leave of this world.

We would remind you that each person has chosen at the soul level for the experience that they will have as these last years tick away. The realities are separating into layers to accommodate everyone's choices and there will be goodbyes all around. You will be saying goodbye to who and how you were, and there will be a period of "floating" between identities, similar to the fetus floating for a time in the womb before it is born. But you need not worry about how you will be provided for. We know your needs and we know what must happen for you to successfully make this transition between this world and the next. It is so important for you to embody TRUST in the process and in the plan for your life. Fear and worries will only hinder you and keep you back, stuck in the old ways and old identity. Let your angels come to you and sing their lullabies of love. You have earned this and it is yours. Enjoy it.

The world that you are leaving will have its time of discord and then all of it will fall silent, too. The old dream is ending and it is time for a new one—for you, for everyone, and for everything. The "refresh button" has been pushed, but it will play out across time, just like the images on your television set or computer monitor are re-drawn one line at a time. There will be a clear sense of something having changed, but it will take time to discover just exactly what it is. In the meantime, relax and let yourselves float upward. It doesn't have to be hard unless you prefer it that way.

Simply let go of the string that ties you to the old ways and let yourself rise up to greet the new ones.

  We are here with you now, in close proximity. We are protecting you as you go through this change. We are guiding you now and will be in touch with you as things unfold for you. You are our "assignment" and most precious to us, and not one of you shall be left behind. If there were some way that you could see us now, you would have no doubt about the love and support being extended to you, but trust in this: the day IS coming when we shall all be together again, and you will know us for who we are—your brothers and sisters in the many mansion worlds of the One Infinite Creator. We leave you now, in peace and honor and blessing. Amen, Adonoy Sabayoth. We are the Hosts of Heaven.

18

THE SPLITTING OF THE WORLDS
February 10, 2001

We have asked to speak to you today because we wish to convey our view of what we see happening at the present time on Planet Earth. We must emphasize that there are many things unfolding simultaneously and the variations at the individual level are infinitely varied and complex, so we can only speak in the broadest and most general terms. However, we feel that it is still worth sharing our perspective with you, so as to provide a context in which you may view what you are experiencing and place your "picture" within our frame.

If you remember, we have spoken before of a splitting off of different future worlds from this one world in which you move and have your experience. Each person has their destination, chosen for them by their soul, in keeping with their place in the larger Divine Plan. For those of you who are inclined to want to heal and fix things, it can be difficult to witness the playing out of the "scripts" that are not of your vibration and orientation. There is an intensification of essence taking place, so that those whom you might consider evil, or selfish, or greedy will appear to become more so, and those who are not able to surrender and bow to the winds of change will surely break from their rigidity. The winds of change are already blowing hard, and they will do so for the rest of the time left for your planet and all upon it. There is no letting up in this birthing process now, so if you are expecting it to pause, know now that it will not.

However, there is good news in this, because it also means that the push toward Terra will not stop, either, and those who are destined for it are being gently lifted into their own vibrational layer (stratum) and that is happening for all of those who are destined for other destinations, as well. There is a layering taking place and the layers are becoming more and more distinct from each other. As this proceeds, the resistance to the movement will be crushed by the relentlessness of the forces toward completion. Those who insist on clinging to the status quo will ultimately be swept away from that which they cling to, but it is all just the way of ensuring that each one ends up fulfilling their life's plan and gets to where they are destined to go.

The slumber is being disturbed, and as things progress, there will come a time when all will awaken to one reality or another. For you who are destined for Terra, you will have a more gentle ride, even in the midst of others' discomfort from their own resistance to change. Nothing will remain of the old at the end of the process, but there is still much time to traverse before that is complete. What you need to know now is to release all attachments to what was in your life and to release all fears for those you love and care about. They will each be provided for in the way that is perfect for them and their soul's choice. We ask that you deepen your trust in the process, for things are going to look pretty extreme in the not too distant future.

There is a limit to the amount of time that you can safely continue to exist in 3D, and we have been instructed from the highest levels as to the logistics involved in making sure that every-one gets to their "right place." You will be sensing the shift as it occurs and do not be surprised by feelings of peace and bliss that come seemingly "from out of the blue," with no apparent external cause. Just relax into them and enjoy them, as eventually they will be your permanent state. These interludes will come more often for you as things progress, and gradually will become the dominant state of your being. You will begin to be able to tell the difference between the state you want to experience and the state that you experience when you engage in old patterns of relationship and communication.

Your body will tell you when you are engaging with dissonant energies because you will experience momentary discomfort that will contrast strongly with this other state of peace and bliss. When you notice this, gently disconnect and redirect your attention to the things you would like to experience and create, rather than the things you would like to stop or oppose. You will find it harder and harder to maintain your connection to things that are not "yours." If you can relax into receiving the lifting, it will go much easier for you. If your personality traits make it hard for you to "let go and let God," then you will have a little help energetically, to pry your fingers loose of their grasp on the twigs that you cling to in your fear of letting go. Each of you will have "moments of truth" in which you will simply "see" what is happening and then it will be easy to walk away from your former battles.

You see, despite what your physical senses register, your inner, subtle senses can give you another view. Even if you look with physical eyes at the world around you, notice that you do not have as much a feeling of being part of what you gaze at, but rather more and more you will feel like you are witnessing something that you don't quite comprehend. That is part of the process of disengaging from what is familiar to you and receiving what is coming to you. There is nothing wrong with you and you are not losing your mind or sanity. You might question why you don't feel as strongly about things that used to seem important to you, but if you can just let it all go, and let yourself feel the peace and bliss that is available, it will be much easier for you to move to your proper layer of vibration. Just seek your "homing frequency" and let everyone else do the same. No one is "wrong" in being the way they are. They are just being WHO they came to be and are experiencing what they came to experience. That is why everything "exists" in the first place—so that the Creator can experience Itself through its many creations, all interacting with each other in infinitely complex ways.

There will be things playing out on the world stage that, given your values and orientation, you could consider horrible. We would say to you to let yourself witness these things but also know that they are not "yours." If you feel an inner "push" to help or "do something," by all means follow that to wherever it takes you, but also do not feel guilty if you do NOT feel intuitively that there is a need to respond. Each person has their part to play and no two are alike. That is why it is so important for you to meditate and spend some time every day in that altered state in which you disengage from the world around you and go within, to that very private place where you only have yourself and your God to contend with.

Create your own sense of sacred space within yourself and draw upon the sustenance that offers to you. You are most "responsible" when you take full responsibility for yourself and your actions and thoughts. You have only your God to "account to." All the "rules" you were taught and may have accepted are null and void for the journey to Terra. You can know intuitively in each and every moment what is the most "right" action or course in that moment for YOU. You are sovereign beings and you are the only one you are responsible for. Everyone else has the same responsibility as yours—to be fully responsible (and responsive) to their own inner urgings, and to fully experience being who and what THEY came to experience.

Most of you who are reading this have not been the "obedient" kind for most of your lives, except if it was to "get along" with others or to please those toward whom you felt some debt or obligation. Now your greatest service is toward fulfilling your own destiny, for you are those who will create the incarnational opportunities on Terra so that others may enjoy that world, also. You are leaving this field of endeavor in order to cultivate another, to shape and enjoy another "garden" in another place and time, and to make for the telling of an entirely new story. It is time for you to accept yourselves as the pioneers that you are, and to understand that your very differences are the things that equip you best to be the transition team between one world and another. Go within and you will find your way along your path, one step after another, and one day soon, you will lift up your heads and behold a new horizon, unlike any that you have ever gazed upon before.

As the world splits apart into the different layers that will go toward their different destined locations, focus on what is yours and let others around you do the same. Most of you are tired of waiting for something better. Well, there is something better and it is arriving now, inside of you, and is unseen except by your "inner eyes." It will feel like a dreamlike state and you will not be aware of anything but what you are experiencing in that moment, just as you would in a dream while you were asleep. But this dream is real and you are just waking up into it, and things will never be the same for you again.

We leave you now in peace and honor and blessing. We shall speak to you again. Amen, Adonoy Sabayoth. We are the Hosts of Heaven.

19

THE BOTTOM LINE
February 25, 2001

We have asked to speak with you today because there are some things happening that we felt we should comment upon. The first thing, however, is to ask you to ask yourselves just how you feel about the information we have offered to you so far. Does it make sense to you or does it just sound like a nice idea that would be VERY NICE if it were true, but you just aren't sure how you feel about it otherwise?

Let us back up a little and recap and summarize the statements we have made in the previous Messages. First of all, this information is only intended for those whose soul/Oversoul choices are aligned with the journey to Terra. There are many other paths available and they will be taken by the overwhelming majority of people who are incarnate on Earth at this time.

Second, the lifting we have spoken of is dependent on one action and one condition alone: it is necessary to have love in one's heart and in order to do that, it is necessary to "root out" (eliminate or neutralize) fear within oneself. We have defined love in part as the absence of fear, so it is only logical that the cultivation of love requires the removal of fear. Nothing else matters. It does not matter what you know about spiritual matters. It does not matter what you look like or what your age is or where you live. What is in your heart and your attendant frequency are the only criteria for the lifting. If you are afraid to receive the lifting for any reason, you will not be lifted.

Third, we are not "rescuing" you. We are here with you to facilitate your process, but you and you alone are responsible to tend to what is yours alone to do. There are things that you can do to make it easier for yourself, and we can give a certain degree of aid when asked, but facing down your fears within yourself is something that you must do for yourself. All of you who have made the soul choice for Terra have also given yourselves the proper "character traits" to be able to do this. Many, if not most, of you have been seeking "truth" all of your life. Most of you have felt different from the others around you and even now do not know many like yourselves. That will all change in time, for in time—when the splitting of the worlds is complete—you will only be in the company of others like yourself, but for now, you are all in various stages of splitting off from those who will follow paths other than your own.

Fourth, on the timeline that leads to Terra, the present Earth will "pass away" and will no longer support life of any kind. It will be barren and totally inhospitable to all forms of life for a very long time, but that is by Divine design and all things will go to their "right place," according to that design. Terra already exists, pristine and untouched except by love. On Terra only love, peace, and joy will exist. That is why you must have love in your heart and not fear, because only that which is of love, peace, and joy will be permitted to enter Terra. There will be a time of transition on our ships, as none of you will be completely finished with your own transformation when the time of lifting arrives, but you must have cleared out enough fear and the fear-based responses (such as anger, judgement, and greed) to be able to be lifted into the ships when that time comes.

Fifth—and this is the hardest part of all for many of you who feel the pull and yearning for the peace, joy, and love that Terra embodies and represents—there is nothing to "fix" about present day Earth. There is nothing to "create" on present day Earth, except to create the peace, joy, and love within yourselves and within your lives to the degree that you can. There is not going to be an organization to join or create that will take you there. There will not be phenomena such as etheric or physical ships or cities until the time comes for the lifting, and then only those who have qualified by their frequency will even perceive them. Anyone reporting those things or predicting those things belong to another path. It is valid for them and it is valid for those who are drawn to those things, but they are not part of the journey to Terra.

There is a state of growing expectation on all fronts now. The power elite are moving forward with their plans, which they expect to complete in the near future. The various religions and organizations have their expectations about what their path holds for them, and they may in fact experience what it is they expect, just as the many groups who have expectations of another kind will most likely experience what it is that they expect to experience. It is all in Divine Order, and each is finding "their own"—their own people and their own actions and their own outcomes. It is all proceeding just as it was created to happen by the choices made at the Oversoul level for those individuals and their particular life experiences.

Therefore, for those whose path leads to Terra, the only things that are appropriate are those that increase one's frequency and decrease one's fears. Meditation will help and will certainly aid in discerning what it true for oneself, but it is not an absolute requirement. It is not necessary to follow elaborate rituals or practices of any kind. Simply placing one's attention on one's breath as it moves in and out is sufficient, and simple prayers of the moment, spoken from one's heart, are more effective than any memorized words, rituals, or formulas can ever be. It is the sincerity and the "heartfelt" quality that holds the power, not the words, and one does best by pausing a moment to FEEL what it is that one truly wants to occur. Then, when the words are chosen, they more nearly reflect the will of the heart and not the mind, and that is where the true power lies.

The journey to Terra is a real one. It is logical that, if indeed this Earth is to pass away, there must be some mechanism to physically transport and sustain the seed stock for Terra before the final cataclysms eradicate all life on the present Earth. While many will indeed incarnate on Terra from the realm of spirit, there must be some mechanism provided to house their developing bodies. There will still be physical births on Terra, very like the births on Earth, only without the pain and without the loss of consciousness that accompanies births on Earth.

We can say unequivocally that until it is time for you to be lifted—whenever that is for you as an individual—none of the phenomena and none of the organizations will get you there. When it is your time to be lifted, the moment will be very clear to you. There will not be any doubt or question in your mind, and there will not be anything leading up to it other than the internal sense of impendingness—nothing external to you will reveal its approach. The journey to Terra is made up of sovereign beings, and true sovereignty means the willingness to be truly who you are and allow everyone else the same privilege. The only authority is one's own relationship with Spirit. No creed, no method, no technique, no material creation or alliance of any kind will do it. You are each like individual lightning rods, grounding the Light of Spirit into the Earth and supporting the lifting of the planet and yourself at the same time. Lightning rods do not work in bundles. They each serve where they are placed.

That does not mean that you should not reach out in love and support to others, but it does mean that each of you must make this journey on your own, within yourself, and with the willingness and bravery that that entails. You will be pioneers and create a new world and like all pioneers, you will be exploring territory that has not been mapped by others who have gone before you. Therefore, even though there is a core of wisdom to be found in all spiritual and religious traditions, you would do well to put those teachings from the past where they belong: in the museums and libraries that are set up to house the relics of the past. Yours is a new world, a new creation, and the only things that will survive the shift are those of essence, not of history and the energies acquired through the passage of time on Earth. ALL cellular memory from Earth lifetimes will be erased. You will be wholly new, in all respects, and you will become this way without passing through physical death.

It is difficult for you to imagine how this could be and what it will be like, so we suggest that you focus instead on the task at hand: face down your fears; remain grounded in the present moment and listen to the voice of your intuition as to how you should respond in each and every moment, and surrender up everything else.

We leave you now, in peace and honor and blessing. Amen, Adonoy Sabayoth. We shall speak to you again.

NOTE: In response to a question regarding the appearance of ships (I myself have seen them) at this time, I received the following response (Feb. 26, 2001):

"We apologize if our statement has caused any confusion. We wish to emphasize that THE SHIPS THAT WILL LIFT PEOPLE OFF THE PLANET as part of the journey to Terra will not be seen until the time of the lifting. That does not mean that some people will not have experiences with ships before then. It only means that those who are reporting seeing ships or who are predicting mass landings or the like are not referring to the ships which will take one to Terra.

Amen, Adonoy Sabayoth. We are the Hosts of Heaven."

Also, with regard to the erasure of cellular memory, it is my understanding that only the EMOTIONAL CHARGE associated the data is neutralized. The data is always available and is a permanent part of the hologram/Akashic record, but without the charge, one is not usually drawn to revisit those experiences. There is an abundance of things appearing in the eternal "now" and that's where one's fascination lies.

FAQ

ANSWERS TO
FREQUENTLY ASKED QUESTIONS

Q. Will a person know when they are going to "be taken"?

A. Yes, in most cases. The only exception to this will be if a person has been preparing and there is a "surprise" that requires us to lift them physically in order to take them out of harm's way.

Q. What will happen to those we leave behind (families, friends and pets)? Will we need to make preparations beforehand? What will they experience? Will we just disappear from their world? Will they remember our having been there?

A. They will be provided for on an individual basis. Each case is unique, but if you need to make preparations (in keeping with your commitments), you will know it at the right time. This may not come as "words in your head," so much as a FEELING that "it is time to ..." (whatever is right for you to do). What their experience will be depends on their particular life script, what they are supposed to experience in the playing out of their soul's design for their life.

Q. You say that Terra is already there, and that third-density Earth will lie fallow for a long time. If Terra is already there, why do we have to go somewhere else after we are lifted from the planet?

A. You will have to go through an intermediate process before YOU are ready for Terra. Terra is ready, but she is in a frequency band that requires those things that occupy her to be at the same frequency, what is sometimes called the "Christ consciousness" or "cosmic consciousness" level of awareness. Each level of awareness has a natural resonance with a particular frequency band. You are being raised to an intermediate level, so that you can be taken aboard one of our very large mother ships. There, we have total control of the environment and can phase you through the rest of your process in a wholly safe manner, without the need for you to provide for yourselves and your everyday needs. You will be provided with all the assistance you require to complete your shift into full mastery and the reclamation of your full powers. You will also need to adjust to the higher-density way of doing things, so this environment will act as a sort of "halfway house" to enable you to complete your preparations to colonize Terra.

Q. I have heard people talk about going to the fifth dimension, but you say we're going to the fourth density. What is the difference between density and dimension, and why the different numbers?

A. A dimension is a vector quantity. It measures the distance from one point to another along a line. When you speak of a package, you say it has dimensions of so many inches—length, height, and depth. Those are the 3 *dimensions* of space. But you experience yourselves as moving through time, so you are inclined to say there are 4 dimensions to your third density experience. Time actually has 3 dimensions, also, but that is the stuff of those who deal with such mathematical and physics problems as the curvature of time. It takes the 3 dimensions of time to express a point on a curved surface. Your *experience* of linear time is of moving along a single line from the past, through the present, into the future. Therefore it is naturally reflected in your common language as a single dimension, which represents or refers to your position along that single line.

Therefore, if (in common parlance) one speaks of having 4 dimensions in third density, one can view going to fourth density as having 5 dimensions, the added dimension being the eternal "now," the holographic "capsule" that contains your focused awareness of your unfolding experience. You could look upon the fifth dimension as a sphere, in which you can slide back and forth along that single line of "past, present, and future" like a bead on an infinitely long string.

Density is a measure of material reality. It is a measure of how closely packed the particles are that make up a given substance. For example, if one considers water in its solid state (ice), the molecules of water are tightly packed and locked into a lattice. They vibrate relatively slowly. When enough energy is supplied to the system, the bonds between the molecules break and the molecules are free to move past each other. They vibrate faster now. This is the liquid state you call water. If more energy is put into the system, the molecules separate even further apart and move freely through the containing medium ("air"). They move very quickly now. In this state you call the water "steam" or "water vapor." You can see and feel the ice and the water, but not the water vapor, except as a subtle sensation of "humidity." This is a good analogy for what is happening to you now. You can see and feel your material reality, but not the less dense reality that is the next step up from your present environment, except as a subtly-sensed feeling of "presence."

When density (the degree of packing) is combined with gravitation, you get "weight." If you can nullify gravitation, you are "weightless." The total *mass* is the same, but the weight changes with the strength of the gravitation. People who can nullify the gravitation can levitate or act on material objects with their minds so that the objects can float or move through space. When we are on board a ship of ours, we link our consciousness with that of the ship (all matter is conscious) and simply "project" ourselves AND the ship to our intended location. You call this psychokinesis. It comes with the package of powers that one has in full mastery over the material plane. The level of consciousness is the key. When one is in eternal Union with the Creator, one has a direct link to full control over material reality. One also has the WISDOM for the "right use" of such abilities.

As your frequency rises, more energy is contained in your system. In our water example, when there is enough energy in your system, the water becomes "invisible" to those molecules (and the tissues and organs that are made of them) which are operating at the "solid" and "liquid" states. Just so with your becoming invisible to those who are operating at the more dense levels of material reality. When we say your frequency has risen, your molecules have absorbed more energy and are moving more quickly. They eventually move so quickly that they are invisible to the sensory tissues of those who are vibrating (moving) more slowly. That is why you will become invisible to those who are not at the higher frequencies. That is why you cannot see us now, but you will be able to see us when you have absorbed enough energy to vibrate in the same frequency range as we do.

As to your question regarding the different numbers, it is just a matter of which system of nomenclature you are using. We use the system of densities, which to us is a more accurate way of describing the particular band of material reality that we are referring to. There is the whole separate issue of the different "planes" of reality. There is space/time and time/space. They are analogs of each other. Each density has this pairing, but the difference is most pronounced at third density. In third density, there is the space/time plane that you experience in your normal waking consciousness, and there is the time/space analog that is called the "astral plane." When one is operating in the normal pattern of third density, there is interchange between these two, only they are separated by a "veil" or barrier such that one can only access the astral plane under certain conditions, one of which is the phenomenon you refer to as physical death. People commonly refer to the astral plane as the "fourth-dimension," but this is not accurate. Calling time the fourth dimension is not really accurate, either, but it at least expresses an aspect of third-density reality that approaches the actual situation of the *experience* of third density.

There is much confusion about these terms, especially in the metaphysical field and the so-called "New Age" parlance. We prefer clarity to confusion, so we use the term density rather than dimension. We are referring to a particular frequency band in the spectrum of the Creation, along with its attendant forms and available functions. We have noted before that "form follows function." Each frequency band has its appropriate forms that outpicture the available functions. In third density, the level of consciousness (frequency) is such that the available functions are more limited. When one moves up the spectrum, more functions become available and the forms change to reflect that. You will appear as "gods" and "goddesses" because your range of available functions (powers) will appear truly "godlike" when compared with those of third density.

Q. You said that some of us will be coming back to assist. From what you have just said, that implies that we will either be "invisible helpers" or will have to lower our frequency to be visible. If we lower our frequency, wouldn't we lose our powers?

A. Once one has attained a state of permanent Union with the Creator, it is permanent. One has total control over the material plane, and can come and go from it at will. However, one is not likely to remain there longer than necessary to perform a particular task or series of tasks. When the one you call Jesus had attained the fourth-density state, he came and went for 40 days, to prove to his followers that he still existed. He appeared in what looked like a physical body, and ate and drank to prove its materiality. He did so to make a point that was in keeping with his larger mission. When one is in that state of consciousness, one always knows in the moment what is the single most appropriate choice or action. There is absolute clarity. In a world based on doubt and fear, it is difficult to imagine a world based on love and wisdom, but that is where you are going and that is what Terra is like. We would remind you that our definition of love includes the absence of fear and the presence of trust in the Creator. When you are in love and wisdom, there is no fear or doubt.

Q. You said we would be "taken to another place." How exactly will that occur?

A. It will happen in exactly the right way and the right time for each individual. For those of the first wave, it will probably consist entirely of rising in frequency until one simply is "there." For the second wave, there will be a mixture of methods used, since some of those will have to be lifted physically into our ships, while others will be able to shift frequencies. For those of the third wave, they will be lifted in their physical bodies at the last possible moment, for they will not be far enough along in their spiritual process to make the frequency shift from within third density. We have all the bases covered, and each one will experience what is theirs to experience in exactly the perfect way. Remember, these decisions are made at the soul/Oversoul level, so you will all be standing on the right dock when it is time to board your ship for the next phase of the journey.

Q. The Heaven's Gate cult referred to "the next level above human," and expected to be taken aboard spaceships also. How is this different from what they were talking about, and why did they leave their bodies behind?

A. We cannot answer that question fully, for to do so would breach a "rule" of noninterference. They have passed on, and we can assure you that they did exactly what they came to do. There are no accidents. However, since there is widespread speculation (among those who are still walking around in third density) as to whether they committed suicide, were murdered, or did indeed link up with a space ship associated with Comet Hale Bopp, we cannot tell you exactly what happened there or we would infringe upon or affect your process.

However, we *can* tell you how THIS series of Messages and information relates to that group and their experience. First of all, that group evolved from the personal energies of two people. They lived together, traveled together, and gave their power to those two individuals to the extent that they followed their every order and directive, right to the end. The group also changed over the course of 20+ years. The original teachings were rather pure, and dealt with what is commonly termed the process of "ascension." The individual you call Jesus, as well as certain other historical figures, ascended. They left the Earth plane (third density) IN their bodies. They "took their bodies with them." However, one can also "ascend" from a disembodied state. In a case like that, one leaves the body behind, and completes the ascension to the next level of consciousness while in an astral body.

The *original* teachings of the two leaders of the group had 3 tenets:

1) There is a window of opportunity for the movement to the next level of consciousness, after which the window closes.
2) If you haven't taken your body with you, you haven't done it.
3) All you can do is to prepare yourself to receive the experience. When the moment arrives, the missing ingredient is supplied "from above." You cannot make this happen on your own.

There is an obvious similarity here to some of what we have been saying, but there are some key differences, also. It should be noted that after the group had gone on for so long, the end result was not in keeping with the original tenets upon which the group was formed. Things change, and so did both the focus and the function of that group. You have seen the apparent result, but which of you knows what REALLY happened? You can only speculate, and we have to leave it that way.

However, we can distinguish between the beliefs and actions of that group and these Messages in several ways. First of all, there is no "group" here. There are no "leaders" to follow. We have asked Lyara to deliver this Message for us and she continues to serve as our microphone into your reality through these communications. However, that is as far as it goes. None of you are being asked to leave your homes, to follow anything but the prompting of your own guidance, the "still, small voice" within you. We have not asked you to go through austerities, only to give your spiritual practice the highest priority in your life. We have not asked you to master all of your human emotions, to give up your sexuality, or to otherwise reject your human experience. We have only asked you to do what is right for you *as an individual* to do. There is no "group" here except that of a "soul family." We are your brothers and sisters in the many "mansions" of the heavens. We are the "hosts" of "heaven" and we are inviting you to join us in a wonderful banquet, a homecoming party, in which you will re-attain what you had before you embarked on your service to Planet Earth at this time.

There IS a "next level above human," and Terra is where you will express and experience that. We are taking you aboard our ships in the ways that best fit your individual circumstances, soul choices, and place in the overall plan. You are either going to resonate with this material or you will not. It is a matter of what you are made of, who you are, and what allegiance and loyalty you have. We will make one last observation. None of you who are part of Operation Terra will go through physical death. You will be taken aboard our ships, complete your transformation, and be prepared to occupy Terra. You will leave behind all the baggage of your old identities, for nothing of the old will be taken into the new. This will be a totally new beginning, for you and for the planet, a time to truly create "Heaven on Earth." We look forward to having you among us again.

We leave you now, in peace and honor and blessing. Amen, Adonoy Sabayoth. We are the Hosts of Heaven.

SUGGESTED READING

Itzhak Bentov, *Stalking the Wild Pendulum: On the Mechanics of Consciousness*, reprint edition. Inner Traditions Ltd. 1988

David Bohm, *Wholeness and the Implicate Order*, reissue edition. Routledge, 1996.

George M. Lamsa, *Holy Bible: From the Ancient Eastern Text, George M. Lamsa's Translation from the Aramaic of the Peshitta*. Harper San Francisco, 1985.

James M. Robinson, *The Nag Hammadi Library in English*, reprint edition. Harper San Francisco, 1990.

Baird T. Spaulding, *Life and Teachings of the Masters of the Far East*, Vols. 1–3. DeVoors and Co., 1983.

Michael Talbot, *The Holographic Universe*, reprint edition. Harper-perennial Library, 1992.

Gary Zukav, *The Dancing Wu Li Masters: An Overview of the New Physics*, reissue edition. Bantam Books, 1994.

ABOUT THE AUTHOR

Sara Lyara Estes, known as "Lyara" on the Web, earned a B.S. in Zoology (cum laude) from the University of Michigan, a Lifetime Teaching Credential (K–9) from California State University, and an MBA in Information Systems from Golden Gate University. She also earned real estate and securities broker's licenses, took 1200 hours of training in energy systems and bodywork at the New Mexico Academy of Advanced Healing Arts, and received formal training in accessing other planes of reality from several teachers, both those on the planet and those above it.

In her work in medical research laboratories, she developed the first reliable method for cloning tissue and identified a previously unknown cell type that proved significant in immunology related to organ transplants. She served as a key research *subject* in the original biofeedback experiments conducted by Dr. Joe Kamiya at Langley-Porter Neuropsychiatric Institute and was also tested for her telepathic abilities in his laboratory, with a success rate of 100%. Walter Cronkite featured her in a *21st Century* segment, "Miracle of the Mind." She also served as Administrative Assistant for Computer Services at Cornell University's Graduate School of Business and Public Administration, as the Training Director for Data Processing for the State of New Mexico, taught sixth grade in Concord, California, and was operations manager for Unisun, a solar energy company in Santa Fe, New Mexico.

In March 9, 1981, Christ appeared in her bedroom, put his hands on her head, and called her to a path that eventually stripped her of every bit of her former life, but which served to strengthen her and soften her at the same time. After being totally disabled by a collapse of her immune system in 1984, she began the long walk back to functionality and turned to writing as one of the few things she could do while living life as a "bubble person," allergic to almost everything. Her articles were published in several New Age magazines, and when she was well enough to work again, she began doing book production services for small publishers and various authors. She now lives in a remote area of north central Washington state, and does Web site development and publishing services for a living.

ABOUT THE PUBLISHER, CONTACT INFORMATION

Celestial Cooperatives has been in the business of providing professional book production services since 1993. These services include editing, proofreading, typography, graphics, book design, and electronic pre-press for publishers and self-publishing authors.

Electronic publishing is a natural outgrowth of print publishing, and Celestial Cooperatives also provides professional Web site development and maintenance for all types of clients, including authors, non-profit organizations, commercial sites, and those who simply want to use the Web as a resource for sharing their views and information.

With the publication of this first volume of the *Operation Terra* material, Celestial Cooperatives has launched its existence as a publisher in its own right, and can consider cooperative publishing ventures in connection with other select titles, provided that the author is prepared to fund the production and printing of the title and the content is an appropriate fit with the particular niche and philosophy expounded in the *Operation Terra* material.

You may contact Celestial Cooperatives at the following locations:

Postal Mail: PO Box 2231-A, Oroville, WA 98844-2231
Phone: (866) 476-8100 (Toll-free for the US); (509) 476-2747
   (Office hours 10 a.m. to 8 p.m., Pacific Time, Mon.–Sat.)
Fax: (509) 476-4989
e-mail: celestia@celestcom.com
Web site: www.celestcom.com